Passport to Missions

Passport to Missions

W. Guy Henderson

Broadman Press / Nashville, Tennessee

4263–15
ISBN: 0–8054–6315–1

Dewey Decimal Classification: 266.023
Subject heading: MISSIONS, FOREIGN

Library of Congress Catalog Card Number: 78–057816
Printed in the United States of America

It's tomorrow too soon.
Home in a hole,
No rice in the bowl,
It's tomorrow too soon.

Author Unknown

Contents

	Foreword by Owen Cooper	ix
	Preface	xiii
1.	What the Bible Says About Missions	21
2.	William Carey Launches a New Day	31
3.	What on Earth Are They Doing Out There?	39
4.	The National Takes a Look At the Missionary	53
5.	What Makes a Good Missionary?	67
6.	When Is Mission Work Actually Being Done?	83
7.	What the National Can Do That the Foreigner Cannot Do	101
8.	Mission Methods You Need to Know	113
9.	The Layman and Mission Support	131
10.	Things That Hurt	143
11.	The Christian Woman on the Mission Field	153
12.	The Layman's Finest Ministry	163
Appendix A	A New Look at Some Old Fallacies	173
Appendix B	Timely Tips for World Travelers	177

Foreword

Outstanding performance has always been a commendable trait of Christian service. The man who does his homework in advance is far more apt to succeed because half of the task is being prepared. When a pastor or a lay person has the opportunity to minister overseas, they need to go prepared. Philip was prepared for his trip to the Gaza desert and it was successful.

I have seen earnest Christians become almost useless and any hope of effectiveness shattered by what they encountered overseas. They became so conscious of the differences in culture that it dominated their thinking. They were confused by the languages, smells, and sounds; battered by the mob of people, and perplexed by the poverty. This book is designed to help the new witness become aware of this. I have also seen the veteran assume such a superior know-it-all attitude with the nationals that they breathed a sigh of relief when he was gone.

For a long time we've needed a book to orient pastors and lay workers to the ways and means of mission activities in another culture. Mr. Henderson's book will not solve all your overseas problems, but many of your questions will be answered. It will set you thinking in a positive direction that will make you thirsty to know more.

It has been my desire for years that more lay persons would be involved in mission work. I don't believe the four walls of a building can contain all that God wants his people to do. There are places in the Jerusalems, Judeas, and Samarias of the world where more church people need to go. How thrilling it is to see pastors and lay persons working in these ventures. It behooves us to do all that is possible to make our message and ministry attractive to other groups when we do go.

Some have discovered that the best remedy for a sick church is to be put on a missionary diet. When our lay people begin moving to our mission fields, they become motivated. There is a greater interest in praying, giving, and going. My own church in Yazoo City is a testimony to this.

Under the leadership of our pastor, James F. Yates, for the past seventeen years, and his predecessors, we have grown a great mission-minded congregation, one that gives 28 percent through the Cooperative Program, makes worthy home and foreign mission special offerings, has involved itself in having a major role in organizing at least twelve churches in the past twenty-five years, and currently is assisting two Mission Service Corps volunteer couples.

No small part of this mission commitment has come from the members of the congregation who have been meaningfully involved in witnessing and congregation-alizing in the United States and in foreign countries.

You have before you a serious attempt to spell out attitudes that will enhance the tug of the gospel. The author has spent twenty years on the mission field and has observed the ministry of many visitors. Most of our missionaries have yearned for some manner of orientation that would help guide one into practical service on a mission field. You may not agree with all that is written but you will still profit by reading it.

In a way it reminds me of the conversation of a man with Charles Alexander. The man said, "I don't like the way you do personal work."

"Neither do I," replied Mr. Alexander. "Tell me, how do you do it?"

"Well, I don't do it at all," was his answer.

Alexander said, "Then I like the way I do it better than the way you are doing it."

There are various ways to do mission work, but perhaps the most important way is to get out there and begin, but begin with a guide book. You will find PASSPORT TO MISSIONS most helpful.

OWEN COOPER
Yazoo City, Mississippi

Preface

Missions is big business. Computerized, transistorized, and energized, it seeks to keep moving toward its goal. Thousands of people are caught up in it. Some are the shock troops out on the cutting edge, others are engaged in writing, promotion, and recruiting. Many more study about missions. Inspired, as in the book of Acts, they give, sometimes even generously. Christian colleges and theological seminaries have answered the challenge and missions has become part of the curriculum.

Today, thousands of lay people are visiting the mission fields. Fast and safe travel has transferred the jet set to the remotest missionary outpost. Usually they are enthusiastic about what they see. Sometimes they are witch-hunting and witches they find. Much hidden for years by tight-lipped missionaries is now quite obvious to the layman. Faults and flaws, sacrifices and service, all will become part of his report.

Foreign missions, at least in its modern garb, began with William Carey in the early part of the last century. Much has been learned about mission mistakes, responsive people, colonialism, and nationalism in the intervening years. This history is vital to our knowledge of missionary activities or we commit ourselves to repeat the same mistakes. And mistakes are to be found. Only in the last few decades has there been a serious attempt to learn why people respond to the gospel and why others are unresponsive. Rampaging nationalism is being felt and the downtrodden are no longer satisfied with the husk of the promised land.

Methods have ever been intriguing. Wars have been fought with sticks and stones and with B-52's and atomic weapons. Thus, the methods of warfare are constantly being revised. This could also be said of missions. The invention of the printing press meant a wholesale change in mission methods, and this was just the beginning. Now there is a call for television repairmen, pilots, nurses, agriculturalists, and some sixty other occupations that are open in the global ministries. The message remains the same but our methods of getting it out has gone from the itinerating lone-ranger evangelist to task force, blitzkreig, saturation evangelism. Increasingly, laymen have found places of service on the mission field that give a sense of fulfillment hitherto unknown. Studies have shown that no one method is right for every country. What works well in Indonesia may leave the Spaniard cold. This calls for a high degree of versatility and inventiveness with the gospel by the missionary.

Things can be done by the layman which are extremely helpful. On the other hand, he can become the religious fly in the Third World ointment, playing havoc among the missionaries and the nationals. Communication is a vital link in understanding the layman visiting the field, the professional missionary, and the national. It is hoped that the following chapters will be of service to the veteran world traveler and to the eager layman on his first trip. The first two chapters are designed to present the biblical basis for missions and the early history of foreign missions. Chapter 3 raises the curtain on missions overseas and how the short-term visitor can favorably influence others toward Christ. You may want to begin with chapter 3 if time is short and read the first two chapters at a later time. As you go, go in confidence, go inspired, go with God.

Passport to Missions

Reflection #1

The old Korean man was very uncomfortable in the jeep. I had picked him up in a farming village and offered him a ride into town. His shoes were muddy and he wanted to know if he should remove them before he climbed into the vehicle. This was not his style of going into town, but he would tolerate it. I asked him if he knew anything about God and he nodded his head and said that he had heard of God. Then I asked him if he knew anything about Christ Jesus. "No," he declared, "I have not heard of him. No one has told me and I've not seen it written." Seventy-five years of this farmer's life had passed before he heard about Christ.

" 'How then shall they call on him in whom they have not believed? and how shall they believe in him of whom they have not heard? and how shall they hear without a preacher' " (Rom. 10:14).

1.
What the Bible
Says About Missions

Scientists have discovered that all bodies emit a measure of energy in some degree. This may be barely perceptible to the eye or the touch but still it is there. The Old Testament is like this in a sense of missionary radiation. There is no "go ye" spelled out, but missionary vibes are found in most every book.

The apostle Paul believed this and wrote, "And the scripture, foreseeing that God would justify the heathen through faith, preached before the gospel unto Abraham saying, In thee shall all the nations be blessed" (Gal. 3:8). Paul saw far more in Abraham's call than merely Canaan being blessed. Through him and his seed all nations would share the glory of Jehovah.

The writer of Hebrews felt this missionary radiation and said, "God, who at sundry times, and in divers manners spake in times past unto the fathers by the prophets" (Heb. 1:1). The prophets were revealing more and more of God's plan. It was plain that redemption was the heart of that strategy.

The story of Ruth emphasizes God's plan afresh. Elijah was sent only to the widow of Zarephath, a foreigner, though Jesus said there were many widows in Israel at the time (Luke 4:25–26).

Jonah, who had little love for foreigners, was sent by the Lord to proclaim repentance unto them. Prejudiced, narrow-minded, and blinded by God's blessings to Israel, Jonah was unable to convince himself that repentance and salvation could be extended to outsiders. He ended up at ease under the shade of a gourd vine. His anger was multiplied when it withered. God used this to teach him that he had compassion on the gourd vine, which he did not make nor have any special interest in. Now says Jehovah, "Should not I spare Nineveh, that great city?" (Jonah 4:11). The entire book stands as a rebuke to the Hebrew nation for their failure to share the message with other nations. Even the great wicked cities of the world are loved by God.

In Psalm 67 the writer declares, "All the ends of the earth shall fear him" (v. 7). Note that "nations" not nation, and "peoples" not just people are mentioned. In Psalm 96 all the earth is to worship God and the entire world will accept his righteous rule with joy and thanksgiving.

Daniel stands, forever recorded, as a foreign missionary in the highest sense. His courage, prayer life, and witnessing should inspire missionaries everywhere.

Isaiah believed in this missionary radiation and prophesied saying, "And the Gentiles shall come to thy light and kings to the brightness of thy rising" (Isa. 50:3). God's plan, like the rising of the sun, is revealing more and more. The early Old Testament writers could dimly see the missionary purpose, but in the dawn's early light, they were able to see tribes, nations, and people.

Jesus Christ and Missions

In "the fulness of the time," he came (Gal. 4:4). The prophets had written of his coming and the Hebrew nation, coming from the furnace of affliction, cradled the Son of God. The Greeks had a magnificent language to express his teachings. The Romans had conquered the world and given a stability and a political climate that would enable the gospel to reach throughout the empire. His teachings would be as "never man spake like this man" (John 7:46). His healing would express a depth of concern that would inspire men forever. His love would break down barriers and say to men, "The fields . . . are white already to harvest" (John 4:35).

Christ declared that "God so loved the world" and that forgiveness was for every man. His parables opened doors in the minds of men revealing that "A king prepared a great supper and ordered his servant to invite many."

The ninety and nine were safe but one was lost.

A father welcomed *both* sons to come inside.

The good Samaritan served while others walked by, and Christ commanded, "Go, and do thou likewise."

Christ announced that it was unwise to put new wine into old wineskins. The new wine of the gospel would not fit into the ragged wineskin of Judaism. God's love and grace was an expanding, growing process and the old traditions would not contain it. It would leap barriers, cross color lines, speak to male and female, Jew or Gentile, in this expansion.

He announced his suffering, death, and resurrection, and the forgiveness of sin must be preached to all nations. "Ye are witnesses of these things" (Luke 24:28), were his electrifying words to the disciples.

The parting charge of Christ found in Matthew 28:19–20 is the best known commission to the church: "Go ye therefore, and teach all nations, baptizing them in the name of the Father, and of the Son, and of the Holy Ghost: Teaching them to observe all things whatsoever I have commanded you: and, lo, I am with you alway, even unto the end of the world."

Three great facts are underscored. First, he announces that all power in heaven and earth belongs to him. The energizing authority was in the right place. The same power that brought Christ from the grave would be operative in the lives of his followers. Second, his command was to "Go ye," or literally, "as ye go." The task for the church was to spread the gospel by teaching and baptizing, remembering the source of power. Note that Christ said, "Go ye into all the world." The expanding, conquering, dynamic gospel was moving out. Third is the grandest promise, "I am with you alway, even to the end of the world." Countless Christian workers in barren deserts, lofty mountains, or crowded cities could testify to his presence.

The Early Church in Mission Outreach

Christ had kept his promise. The Holy Spirit came empowering the small penniless group of disciples. "Sil-

ver and gold have I none," became the hallmark of
the group. "In the name of Jesus of Nazareth, rise up"
(Acts 3:6), was the cry of victory.

Three thousand responded to that message and were
baptized. Great fear was upon the city and they continued praising God daily in the Temple and from house
to house. What a mission strategy! "Ye have filled Jerusalem with your doctrine" (Acts 5:28), was the accusa-
tion of the chief priest. Small wonder the Lord added
to his church daily. Christianity was more than a Sunday morning, eleven o'clock engagement. It was a vital
union with Christ that daily produced fruit. How poor
is our brand of Christianity if days and seasons, events,
and programs become more important than this daily
walk.

New expanding horizons beckoned to the church.
They were scattered abroad, at least once, by severe
persecution. God would not permit his new wine to
become another Jewish sect in the religious wine vat.
The Galatian church sought to water it down so the
old wineskin would contain it and Paul pronounced
a curse upon anyone seeking to do this. The Jerusalem
Council, in Acts 15, revealed two distinct groups in
the church. Christianity had reached the crossroads.
One group demanded that Jewish rituals be kept. They
refused to follow the clear teaching of the Holy Spirit.
They left the mainstream of Christianity and died out.

Then the gospel broke out of the narrow confines
of Palestine. Churches sprang up in Ephesus, Corinth,
and Philippi. Saints were reported even in Caesar's
very household. It battered at the door of evil and

corrupt religions. The idol business of wicked men was destroyed. The church was on the move. The Holy Spirit called, separating men to be missionaries. The church supported them with prayers and financial gifts. Offerings were sent from one church to help another in need. Letters of recommendation were sent across continents saying, "I commend unto you Phebe" (Rom. 16:1). Runaway slaves were converted and then returned as brothers.

This business was paying the highest dividends ever known. One man declared that all the world was as but refuse in comparison to knowing the Lord Christ. "I shall give thee the heathen for thine inheritance" (Ps. 2:8) was considered worth more than all the wealth of Arabia. Men had once sought to build a tower to heaven and their language was confounded. Now men were proclaiming a new way to heaven and the language was again universal. Knowing Christ meant they had to share that message.

A vital part of missions is to understand God's concept of missions and then to bring our thoughts and our programs in line with that concept. Mission strategy and programs will change but the plan of God remains. Thus we need to bathe our minds in that holy plan of the ages.

From our study of the Bible we can ascertain that God's purpose is clearly stated: to preach the gospel throughout the world, to make disciples and to teach them the Word of God. They in turn are to teach others who will continue to share this message.

Christian missions originated with God. We are to

be his witnesses. People were to fulfill this plan. We are to be laborers together with our Lord. It is interesting to note that Christ called his early disciples from among the common laboring people. Ordained men were available, but he chose to call laymen who would leave the fishing trade or the tax office and follow him.

Missions is not a man-made device for raising money and sending people overseas. It is a divine plan enabling believers to become witnesses wherever they are. Their Jerusalem may be a feed store, a garage, or a bank, but from this Jerusalem their ministry should reach out to the Judeas, Samarias, and to the uttermost parts of the earth. Every child of God can have a part in it. The Holy Spirit has given various gifts to the church, the body of Christ. This body is complete, nothing is lacking.

Men in every occupation need to know Christ and to accept this challenge to engage in a new partnership. A world bound and shackled by evil superstitions, pagan gods, and blinded by Satan could be set free. Men would be able to say, "I was in prison, and ye came unto me" (Matt. 26:36). We have an almighty God, whose purpose, whose power, whose plan, is to reach out with redemptive incarnate love to every man.

Reflection #2

The baby was born but lived only a few hours. The missionary doctor did all he could, but finally the life of the little one expired. The numbness of the moment was upon us. We knew not where to turn, nor what to do. Parents, loved ones, and dear friends were 10,000 miles away. Then, God's grace that is always sufficient became such a vital part of our life.

Missionary friends began to come, some driving all night to get there. National pastors and people were concerned and came to pray and comfort. A friend had a little box made and lined with white silk for the coffin. The Presbyterian Mission had the only foreigner's cemetery in the area, and these dear friends provided the burial site and wept with us. A fellow missionary read the Scripture, another spoke the words of comfort, and then in a lonely corner of the cemetery we buried part of us. Later, a simple monument would be added. I could not help but think of all the monuments that had been erected across Asia, or Africa, or South America, and the tears that had watered the sod.

Some weeks later, a dear lady of the Woman's Missionary Union sent us a card of sympathy. There was a Scripture verse from Job, declaring that "He gives songs in the night." In that long night through which we had passed, we could still praise him who causes us to rejoice even in the darkest night.

2.
William Carey
Launches a New Day

The nineteenth century, according to religious historians, was the great missionary century. During the Reformation the church was concerned with doctrines and putting their spiritual house in order. There was very little knowledge of the outside world and geographical contact was limited.

Protestant missions in the sixteenth and seventeenth centuries were carried on in narrow confines. In 1634, the city of Lubeck, Germany, sent a missionary to Abyssinia. There were Dutch missionaries in Ceylon as early as 1636. About this time John Elliot was working among the American Indians. However, all of this was sporadic and the church really had little, if any, vision of reaching non-Christian people in other lands.

Moravian missionaries work began in 1732, and Quakers were active in Europe, Asia, and Africa, as well as America. In these opening approaches there was little organization or continuity. Perhaps the most serious drawback was the greed that would characterize those who came after them. Traders, explorers, and navigators questing for gold sailed the seas. Vasco da Gama, Portuguese admiral, rounded the Cape of Good

Hope and opened a new route to India. Soon the British
East India Company was to gain supremacy for England in India, Burma, and other Eastern nations.

Captain James Cook, in his world voyages from 1768
to 1779, aroused a lot of interest in the outside world.
In Kettering, England, William Carey, who was to become the father of modern missions, was greatly interested in the explorations of Captain Cook and others.
He was led to know the Lord by a fellow apprentice
in the shoemaking industry and became a Baptist
preacher. Diligently he studied Latin, Greek, French,
Dutch, and Hebrew. He became interested in world
missions and by his cobbler's bench kept a map of the
world. In 1792, at Nottingham, he preached a powerful
sermon entitled, "Expect Great Things from God, Attempt Great Things for God." On October 2, 1792,
the Baptist Missionary Society of England was organized at Kettering. A few months later William Carey
became their first missionary, appointed to India. The
modern missionary movement was under way.

The East India Company, owned and controlled by
the British, opposed Carey in the beginning. He took
a position as a factory manager, learned the Bengali
language, and began preaching to the workers. Soon
he was translating the Bible into Bengali and other
dialects. In 1801, he was appointed professor of Sanskrit
and Bengali at Fort Williams College in Calcutta.

Carey had early witnessed the "suttee" practice
where the widow would cast herself upon the funeral
pyre of her husband. He spoke out publicly against
this but it was thirty years before it was declared illegal

by the government. He faithfully continued to labor in his adopted land until June, 1834. He died in India at the age of seventy-three, a long way geographically and in mission advancement from Kettering. The courage and vision of Carey had stirred the Christian Church and added a new dimension to her ministry.

Though there were some before him in foreign mission work, Carey was the one who enabled Christianity to turn the corner. Preachers became concerned, laymen were aroused to support missions, and sending boards were organized. Behind Carey more were to follow as the compassion of men was ignited by a world possessed of darkness.

In 1810, Adoniram Judson and Luther Rice presented themselves to the American Board of Commission for Foreign Missions, asking to be sent as missionaries to the heathens. On the way to India both men began studying their Bibles and separately arrived at the idea that immersion was the New Testament mode of baptism. They promptly joined a Baptist church and began work in Burma. Judson labored there for six years before his first convert, and only baptized twenty-two people during his first fifteen years of missionary service. However, today the results of Judson's work can still be seen in the vast number of Baptists among the Karen and other tribes in Burma.

Meanwhile, in 1807, Robert Morrison sailed to China, having been sent out by the London Missionary Society. En route he was asked in a sarcastic manner if he really expected to make an impression upon the idolatry of the great China Empire. "No, sir," he answered, "but I expect that God will."

Then in Africa, Robert Moffatt and his son-in-law, David Livingstone, were planting the Christian flag. Livingstone explored much of the interior of Africa and had a burning desire to see the land converted to Christ. Once the *New York Herald* sent Henry M. Stanley to find him. Stanley trekked through much of East Africa before finding Livingstone at Ujiji on Lake Tanganyika. Stanley was a skeptic, but came to a new faith in Christ as he saw Livingstone's life and dedication to his task.

As these early missionaries learned new languages, they began to translate the Bible. This called for a wider circulation of the Scriptures. The British and Foreign Bible Society came into existence. It is difficult for us to appreciate the joy of a man when he can read God's Word in his native language. These pioneer missionaries paid a heavy price to translate the Bible and then see that thousands were printed and distributed. Could there ever be a more priceless gift presented to a race of people?

This remarkable upsurge in missions has been of great value to all the world. Savage tribes were Christianized and adopted the ways of civilized men. The early missionaries were pioneers in medical work, schools, and even business, farming, and industrial expansion. The fields of geography, ethnology, and sociology received incalculable amounts of materials and research because missionaries were working with unknown tribes and in distant nations. Better farming methods were introduced by the missionaries, and new crops and fruit production proved popular in many areas.

In 1845, the Southern Baptist Convention was organized in Augusta, Georgia. They separated from the Northern Baptists in order to carry on home and foreign mission work through separate boards. The slavery issue had been in the background, and Northern Baptist rulings and decrees were seen as violations of constitutional rights and autonomy. The Southern Baptists proved to be highly flexible and immediately began sending missionaries. In 1847, Matthew Yates and his wife landed in Shanghai, China, to begin their ministry. For the next 102 years Baptists would work in this intriguing nation. Thousands would be converted. Schools, hospitals, and other institutions would be organized. A mighty force of love and sacrifice was unleashed upon this ancient land.

In 1873, Lottie Moon, from one of the "first families of Virginia," was in China to begin work that would affect Baptist giving and going. She spent thirty-nine years in China and died, in Kobe, Japan, on her way back home to America. Her dedication to her Lord and her sacrifice for the people of the "Central Kingdom" continues to be a source of inspiration.

By 1881, mission history was being made in Brazil by the W. B. Bagbys. The work was slow and steady, but today it constitutes the largest group of Baptists working with Southern Baptist missionaries. On another continent, William David accepted the challenge. This courageous man loved the country of Africa, the people, and his work. In 1875, he began his missionary career in Nigeria and worked mightily to bring light into the dark continent.

All of this was not without great sacrifice. There were many heartaches, sorrows, and tombstones en route to their triumphant hour. They went forth preaching, teaching, and healing in the Master's name. In their wake, there would be churches and conventions that would carry on this type of ministry. Thousands of missionaries would follow them, and the Christian flag would wave in almost a hundred countries of the world. The lay worker, pastor, or missionary who goes out today can be assured that he walks in a hallowed pathway of dedicated men who made straight the highway of the King.

Reflection #3

Relief money had been sent over by concerned groups in rather a large amount. The missionary was told to use it to build houses. A recent typhoon and flood had left thousands homeless.

He tried to hire building contractors but nothing could ever be firmly fixed. Finally, he was told he would have to see the pangulo. *While they did not have a labor union, there was a* pangulo *or boss man, who told them when to work.*

The pangulo *readily agreed to get the job done, and since he was all but homeless himself, he would live in the new village. Meanwhile, the poor people were living in battered tents in a sea of mud.*

Soon workers were swarming over the area. Every day the missionary would turn over money for salaries and materials to the pangulo. *At first he tried to do the purchasing himself but the stores would be out of GI sheeting or out of plywood. Strangely enough, the* pangulo *was always able to find the materials, albeit the price was a little more.*

One day the missionary noted one house was much larger and more elaborate than the others. He was told the pangulo *would live there. "No sir," he said, "people gave that money to help the poor, and I'll see that they get it." He accosted the* pangulo. *Work stopped. The poor people would not move into the new houses that were completed. It was like a ghost town, while across the road the tent village remained crowded and was about to collapse. The missionary urged, pleaded, and tried to persuade the people to move. No one* would move into the new houses. The missionary realized that no one would benefit from the new housing unless the pangulo *had his way.*

He went to the pangulo, *told him he was sorry about all the uproar, and asked him to move into the big house. He did. The next day the people of tent city moved into their new houses.*

3.
What on Earth
Are They Doing Out There?

Since the days of the disciples, efforts have been made to convert the world. The early missionaries knew little about the world into which they were sent. It was all new. Think of all the growth and changes that have taken place since the early missionaries went forth. The sciences have developed: anthropology, sociology, psychology, the history of religion, and psychology of religion. Intensive research is done in the field of religious experiences and missionary methodology.

In view of this goal to convert the world, the by-products of Christianity have been little noted nor long remembered. The emphasis placed on the dignity of man, abolishing slavery, decline of the headhunters, no more "suttee" in India (suttee is the ancient practice where a widow would cremate herself on the funeral pyre of her husband), footbinding in China, severe abuse and misuse of children in sweat shops, all felt the power of the gospel before changing. Honesty, the dignity of labor, education, art, music, and the sciences have been greatly influenced by the Christian community. The hostility that first barred Carey and Judson from India has not all evaporated. In the estimate of many people, the sending of missionaries, the conversion of a man from one religion to another, and the imposition of one's creed upon another is sheer folly.

In spite of this, Christianity has had its friends. The study of cross-cultural living, the complex living patterns of varied societies, and the assimilation of new ideas and thought, is enough to stagger the mind of an sociologist. But the missionary moved in, learned a new language, expressed new concepts and ideas, translated the Bible, organized churches and schools, and though blunders were frequent, still managed to bring the Christian message to a pagan society.

Through the years the message has remained the same but the methods are constantly changing. Missionaries probe new ways to break through the cultural barriers of mankind. They take note of the stratification of societies according to caste, aristocracies, economic position, race, religion, and cultural attainment. Both the beggar and the *yangban* could be evangelized in Korea, but seldom by the same method. Therefore, the patter of missionary activity is constantly changing. "The Old Rugged Cross" is being sung to a new tune.

The major emphasis in the ministry of Christ was preaching, teaching, and healing. The early church continued this type ministry and began to enlarge upon it. Today, teaching may cover everything from a scholar in a seminary classroom, to showing a religious film outdoors to the half-naked inhabitants of some Pacific atoll.

Occasionally you hear of the disappointment of some visiting laymen to the mission field who says, "I thought our missionaries would be out every day among the natives, teaching them and passing out gospel tracts. Instead, they go to colleges, as fine as any we have here, and teach graduate students." There are missionaries who daily don the maligned pith helmets and walk the rice paddies, or along mountain streams, witnessing to all they meet. Other missionaries get into a vehicle and drive to a conference where pastors are discussing church problems or some aspect of evangelism. Missionaries with varied spiritual gifts and a multiplicity of talents, have opened new doors and avenues of Christian outreach.

The missionary work of Southern Baptists gives a good view of the variety of missions today. The one hundred thirty-third annual report of the Foreign Mission Board had 2,776 missionaries in ninety countries. They worked with 8,533 churches with 1,071,922 members. In 1977, these churches had baptized a record 98,715 converts. The budget for the year was $62,685,716.13. This is a report of the work, but how was it done?

We need to keep in mind that the major task is church planting. The missionary seeks to help the local group of believers establish a church that will fit the needs of the culture. He has no desire to promote a Western-style, USA brand of church that will not fit into their life-style, even though at times it happens that way. Dr. Winston Crawley, overseas director for Southern Baptists, once said of mission field churches, "Be assured that when you feel at home, they do not." If an American feels at home in a church of another culture, don't rejoice, for probably the poor national feels like a guest in his own church. I remember a service in Mindanao Island, Philippines, that started at least four times. Outside activities, from cockfights to injured children, would claim their attention and everyone would go out to look. Soon we would all return to the nipa benches and the service would start anew. Apparently it upset no one except the foreigner.

Baptists have long held to the independent, autonomous churches cooperating together in associations and conventions. In this framework the missionary seeks to build. Care must be exercised lest the organization become more important than the building of the church. One veteran missionary likened it to a building and the scaffold. Once the building is erected, the scaffold should be torn down. However, in some areas of church building, the scaffold has to remain to hold up the building. Thus, you find a mission field church with ten or even twenty years of history, still being supported by mission funds, or funds coming from outside the membership. When you see this, you can note another building held up by the missionary scaffold. The self-supporting church speaks well for the missionary methodology as well as the stewardship concern of national believers.

Changing society dictates various methodology for the mission program. The preaching of the gospel remains the same but the surroundings are always changing. Currently we see the following emphases being made.

1. *Evangelism and Church Development.*—This is

paramount in most mission organizations. In 1885, the Methodists and Presbyterians began work in Korea. By 1936, there were 18,000 Methodists and 120,000 Presbyterians. More than one missiologist has observed that the Methodists concentrated on institutions and the Presbyterians on church planting. This is an over-simplification, as statistical gathering on most fields is woefully inadequate. In reality, both groups have done a monumental piece of mission work in Korea. Even so, the value of church planting must not be over-looked.

Peter Beyerhaus has declared, "The church is, at one and the same time, the community of the re-deemed and the redeeming community." Christ has no other institution apart from the church for redemp-tive purposes. Early church history is a record of churches being planted in Ephesus, Corinth, Philippi, and other great cities. The church in the community is the body of Christ and is God's agency for evange-lism. We can expect little growth in any mission where church planting is ignored.

2. *The Mass Media—Radio and Television.*—In heavily populated areas, there will be only one mission-ary for every half-million people. What can we possibly do to make an impact? Mass media is one of the an-swers. In 1977, Southern Baptist had forty-two mission-aries assigned to this ministry who reported 42,931 ra-dio broadcasts and 1,091 television presentations in twenty-eight countries. This is a specialized ministry calling for missionaries highly trained in the technical aspects of mass media. Usually running parallel with

this will be the Bible correspondence courses which have made a great impact in the last few years. In most countries this ministry will take a lion's share of the evangelistic budget.

3. *Publications and Book Stores.*—If churches develop and continue a good teaching program then Bibles and attractive literature are needed. Baptist book stores, one hundred and eight in forty-nine countries, are busily engaged in selling Christian literature to churches and to the public. In 1977, they published over six million pieces of literature and some thirty-three million tracts. There are 107 missionaries plus almost 500 nationals working in this ministry.

Karl Marx is reported to have said, "Give me 26 lead soldiers, (an alphabet in type) and I will conquer the world." A missionary to the Muslims, Samuel Zwemer, said, "No other agency can penetrate so deeply, witness so daringly, abide so persistently, and influence so irresistibly as the printed page." Baptists overseas are quick to accept this, as evidenced by the large number of publications.

4. *Medical Work.*—Christ carried on an extensive healing ministry while he was on earth. He introduced new avenues of compassion for man. The total man, mind, body, and soul was important to him. Hungry or sick people make poor hearers of the Word, unless they are "made whole." Thousands, including many high government officials have been healed in mission hospitals. This has made for smoother operations and relationships in certain fields. In 1977, Baptist medical workers treated more than a million patients in twenty-

one hospitals and ninety-four clinics and dispensaries. There are fifty-four missionary doctors and seventy-four nurses, assisting 608 national doctors in this work.

Lately, a hard and often critical eye has been on medical programs. It is expensive, costing Baptists over $1,300,000 in 1977. It is often in competition with local doctors and hospitals, putting the latter in an unfavorable light. When a local government is furnishing its citizens with adequate medical treatment, there's a question as to whether an expensive mission hospital is needed.

The problem of staff, especially recruiting missionary medical personnel, is not an easy one. The missionary doctor makes a tremendous financial sacrifice when he chooses the mission field. Also, the difficulties of keeping abreast of medical advances and technology is a real problem. In spite of this, the medical mission work has a lot in its favor. The Lord still calls medical people and they respond with compassionate hearts. The illustrious history of medical missions is a glowing chapter in mission efforts.

5. *Educational Institutions.*—No sooner is a man converted than we begin to devise means of training him. In some countries the local school system is adequate, so missionaries may have only a seminary or Bible school. In other nations, there may be an extensive educational system operated by missionaries. Some of these are jointly operated and financed by local conventions. Southern Baptists presently have 426 missionaries and 2,466 nationals working in 219 kindergartens, 156 elementary schools, 48 secondary schools, 8 col-

leges and 67 seminaries. Some 92,949 students are being trained in these institutions. Many of these schools are in the process of being turned over to local national bodies. The Foreign Mission Board has wisely discouraged the building of new educational institutions unless there is real overwhelming need.

6. *Benevolent and Social Ministries.*—The appalling poverty of many nations is what will first impress the visitor. The ever-present beggar with outstretched hand, people sleeping on sidewalks, abandoned babies, and social ills of every nature call for a ministry of compassion. Baptists have eighty-seven missionaries engaged in socially oriented ministries. Another twenty-two missionaries are in agricultural work seeking to teach and train farmers in more productive work. Lately, the Foreign Mission Board and various state conventions have responded to disaster areas in a most effective manner.

7. *Administrative Ministries.*—It takes a large group of missionaries to deal with the affairs of the Mission. The relationship to governmental bodies is daily changing and can be a most difficult work. The average mission has a chairman, a treasurer, and a business manager. They are not limited to office work and usually are working in one or more churches.

Cold statistics can never explain the work of the missionary. How can you list the prayer and concern, the heartaches and suffering, the joys and the victories that are part of the missionary's life. I have seen men pray away the night over a grievous problem in the Convention, and reach out a helping hand to a brokenhearted stranger when not one of his own countrymen would lift a finger to aid him. Some have had to turn their backs on aging parents, say tearful good-byes as teenagers return to America, then turn to face an almost insurmountable task, and do it with a joy and serenity that only our Lord could give. Statistics do not give the total picture and yet it is part of it. Presently Baptist missionaries are working as follows:

- 1,626—General evangelism, church planting, and administration
- 426—Teachers
- 186—Medical work
- 107—Publication and book stores
- 51—Student center workers
- 42—Radio-television workers
- 33—Correspondence course workers
- 22—Agriculture work
- 89—Benevolent and social ministries
- 183—Journeymen
- 11—Special project workers

From another view, there are 1,171 married men, 1,171 married women, 240 single missionaries, and 183 journeymen. Many of the married women are not only homemakers but also hold down full-time jobs in the mission. Homemaking itself can be a full-time job in view of primitive shopping areas and long hours in food preparation.

All mission boards recognize that persons are their most valuable asset. Much time, effort, and finances go into the selection, appointment, and training of missionaries. On the field, health becomes an issue. In many places water must be boiled, vegetables cleaned with chemicals before cooking, houses must be screened, and hundreds of other small things done that the average American takes for granted. Often this will cause some degree of separation with the national. He says, "We've been living with unscreened houses and drinking this water all our lives. Why must the missionaries do all these things?"

Adequate medical services, especially pediatricians and orthodontists, are not to be found in many areas. Thus, expensive travel and frequent furloughs become an issue. This is not exactly a new problem as there is some evidence that the apostle Paul had physical ailments and had the beloved physician, Luke, to accompany his missionary band.

Southern Baptists have chosen to divide mission work into two categories, home and foreign missions. We shall deal primarily with the foreign mission work, but this special emphasis is not meant to denote a sign of value nor importance. Most of our churches, and many lay leaders, are familiar with the work of the Home Mission Board. Some have actually shared in this ministry. The work being done in America constitutes a thrilling chapter of dedication and hard work in mission annals. The new innovations and the compassionate response of the home missionaries have added much to our being able to take the gospel to other areas of the world.

In the 1977 report there were 2,830 missionaries under appointment. They worked in a multifaceted program, encompassing the needs of our nation. Many of these programs are in cooperation with state conventions and associations. Perhaps more than any other cause, this group has made "Southern Baptists" a household word across America. The measure of support this brings to the total mission thrust is incalculable.

Presently the Home and Foreign Mission Boards, along with other agencies, are spearheading the new Mission Service Corps. The goal is to enlist 5,000 mission volunteers by 1980, to serve one or two years in a Bold Mission Thrust movement. The service could be either in the United States or overseas. Also, Bold Mission Thrust aims to double our number of foreign missionaries by the year 2,000.

To accomplish our goals, to make an impact on the world, and to take advantage of our resources and opportunities may well call for a degree of sacrifice akin to that of the first century. The finest spirit would be that of missionary Paul, lying prostrate in the dust, saying, "Lord, what wilt thou have me to do?" (Acts 9:6).

Reflection #4

Across the Hadong River the mountains of Cholla Nam Doe could be seen in the face of a sinking sun. A cool wind from the north swept across the churchyard and whistled through the broken windows of the dilapidated church building. I stood there with a heavy heart and contemplated the history of the Hadong Church. Once, some four years before, I had seen the church full of people and after the service some twenty-five young people gathered in the pastor's home for fellowship.

Now dust covered the floor, cobwebs swept over the pulpit and a rampaging wind snatched at the faded Sunday School and tithers rosters along the wall. I scarce heeded the words of the nearest resident, an unbeliever with a bad reputation, as he explained that the children had broken the windows.

"Why?" That was the big question that hammered at my mind. After returning from furlough, I had learned that the pastor had left the village after taking some church funds and another man's wife. After that the church breathed hard for several months and finally died. Now an empty building served as the tombstone for what had once been a thriving church. Surely there must be some other reason. The faith of fifty people might be seriously crippled by the conduct of an immoral man, but it would not completely die. Could it be that their faith was never upon the Rock, but they had built upon the sand? When the hard rain came, the foundation shifted and their house crumbled. Maybe even the missionary had given them the idea that faith is secondary to things. The faith of our people must

be in Christ, the Solid Rock, not in a man, or in relief products, or in the knowledge of Western or Eastern learning. Knowing that trials and temptations will test their faith severely, we must help them ever to "look unto Jesus."

Dejected, I walked away from Hadong that day. Unlike before, there were no hymns, no prayers, no accompanying believers to see me to the jeep; just the sound of a mournful wind sweeping through an empty church.

4.
The National Takes a Look
At the Missionary

A few years ago the word *native* fell upon hard times. It was a mark of colonialization and exploitation. Visions of half-naked savages, painted faces, and nose bones for cosmetic effect, came into view. The term "national" was then introduced and is widely accepted today to denote the inhabitants of a given area. With the rising tide of nationalism today, there may be an increasing effort to change again. Who wants to be called a "national" of America, or of Kenya or of Thailand? However, in a mission context, we use it to denote the people living in a particular nation.

To understand how the nationals look at missions, we first need to understand what is taking place in the world today. "Tense" may be the best descriptive word of the feelings of today's world. This is not all bad. A little tension can be a good thing, as evidenced by the violin strings. However, some foreboding clouds have been sighted on the horizon and Joe World is concerned.

Runaway Population

Today's world is concerned with people growing at the rate of seventy-four million per year. Projected

world population for the year 2000 is four billion.
Frightening statistics can be rolled off, leaving the
thinking man confused and fearful. We are bombarded
with figures on growth, famine, pollution, and destruc-
tion. Some one hundred and sixty thousand new faces
appear at the world's breakfast table each day. More
land for housing means less land for farming. Jobless,
hungry, and with national resources disappearing or
being polluted, Joe World considers this and he becomes frustrated and tense.

Polarization

This is the attraction of one position as it pits itself
against another. East against West, Communism *versus*
the free world, the oil users against the oil sellers, unde-
veloped nations against the developed nations, and the
list could go on. The inequity of population, two thirds
in the Far East and Southeast Asia, and the West con-
trolling more than three fourths of the world's wealth
is a real sore spot. America, with 6 percent of the population and an estimated 40 percent of the world's
wealth, raises many questions. Africa is increasingly
seeing the white man as the enemy. Latin American
nations continue the tendency to oppose American
economic power. The missionary is often caught up
in this political whirlwind.

Rapid Communication

A boxing match seen around the world simulta-
neously, a riot in Africa watched live in America, a
presidential inauguration flashed across the screens of

the world are all accepted today as commonplace. Satellites and communication procedures are making America's backyard known to the crowded world. The boat, two cars, small family units, spacious lawn, and the grilled streaks have not gone unnoticed. I have often been amazed when a national asks me some minute problem about the United States, and then discover he is well-acquainted with the personalities and the issues involved. American movies, television, and programming is watched in much of the world. The violence, the sexual revolution, and the profanity are viewed and often imitated. The Mafia, Watergate, Lockheed scandals, and other political issues are discussed in great detail. The visitor overseas must be prepared to discuss these issues.

Religion

The world is always concerned about religion. Islam, thanks to the oil-hungry world, is experiencing a revival. After 150 years of mission work in Asia, still only 2 percent of the people are Christian. Japan, with missionaries since the mid 1800s has only one Christian for every one hundred people. There seems to be an important relationship between America's foreign policy and the growth of mission work. Admiral Perry opened the door to Japan and the missionaries moved in. Korea and the Philippines have excellent records of church growth, basking in the sun of a favorable spirit between the United States and these nations. Now with the oil crisis, the rise of nationalism, and a new religious tolerance, much favoritism is being

shown to Muslims. Often the patriotism and religion
of a country will go together. Thus, to forsake such a
religion is the same as being a traitor to your country.

There is another side to this coin. Nationals have
been forced to examine their faith. Is it based on friendship with the United States or upon the Word of God?
Even Muslims have become more interested in outside
religions.

Political Revolution

Since 1950, more than thirty new African states have
been created. The United Nations bespeaks the power
of the Third World. China, closed since 1949 to foreign
missionaries, has been a seething caldron of revolution-
ary forces. North Korea, Vietnam, Laos, and Cambodia
have drunk freely from this fountain. Burma, the land
of Judson and so many Baptists, has the "no welcome"
sign out to missionaries. India and Bangladesh, forever
concerned over castes and religion, are hard to enter.
Malaysia has said "go" to the missionary, and his return
is unlikely. A wary eye is kept constantly upon fifty
nations, or more, that could experience some kind of
revolution tomorrow.

Naturally this has not left the missionary untouched.
They are welcomed on a scale that reaches from sub-
zero to warm.

The National Views the Missionary

"Why should I welcome a rich American missionary
to bring a new religion to my country? We already

have a time-honored religion," said the Chinese businessman.

"You could do more good if you turned over all the money, including the missionary's salary, to the national church. We could spend it more wisely," declared a Korean pastor.

"Yes, yes," said the Japanese leader, "the missionary is welcome, but he must come willing to work under the leadership of the Japanese."

In these statements we can see the national saying, *no, maybe,* and *yes,* usually with a qualifying statement. Samuel Akono, African churchman, writing in the *Crusader* magazine said, "The missionaries have done a tremendous work, but they have made mistakes. They imposed their way of life on us without our consent or approval. We could only sit and stare at what the missionary did. They built schools, hospitals, and farming centers. But, interestingly enough, the missionaries were always the principals, doctors, and engineers at these places. Africans were encouraged to watch what the missionary did."

Pastor Akono is still open to the coming of missionaries and declared that young missionaries are needed who will not come in a spirit of colonialism but in a spirit of brotherhood. We need to listen closely to his plea for men who are not coming to change everything, but to work hand in hand with African churches.

D. T. Niles seeks to sum up the feeling of Asians by saying, "In Asia, missionaries are needed and invited but are not wanted." The missionary has been outmatched in creative planning, outsped to today's frontier, and outlived in pioneering spirit. He is considered by some to be a relic of bygone days. If this can be considered a serious summary of the Asian feeling toward the missionary, indeed it is time we took drastic action. Today, it takes more than just a willingness to "stay put" to be an effective missionary.

Meanwhile, Bishop Stephen Neill has written that, "Christian history has been written far too much from the side of the operators, and far too little from that of the victims. We know fairly well what it feels like to be a missionary. We know far less of what it feels like to be the object of the missionary's attention" (*Call to Mission*, Fortress Press, 1970).

This is enough to make one wonder about the missionary enterprise altogether. However, we need to get a total picture and then come to grips with the problem. It is true that mistakes were made by early missionaries and have been bequeathed to each succeeding missionary. We would have to plead guilty to much of this. Most assuredly, they were doing what they felt to be the best thing at that time.

Still much of the frustration appears to be with America in general rather than with missionaries. It is interesting to note that you will usually hear four questions being asked by nationals on most every field.

1. Why is American home life crumbling if you are a Christian nation? If there are two divorces for every five marriages, isn't the moral fiber of the nation coming apart?

2. Two great world wars have originated in the West. Why?

3. We are confused by your racial discrimination. How can this be? Do you have a caste system?

4. You have many denominations. How can we know which is best?

Many national believers ponder these things, and since the missionary is at hand, and is an American, it is natural that much of his hostility would be aimed at him.

Juan Isais has one of his characters, Dilia, speaking about missionaries in a Latin American country.

First, the missionaries forgive but they never forget. They always remember the offense we have done to them. Second, the missionaries always suspect the nationals of some kind of moral weakness or unfaithfulness, and never believe that Christ, who began a good work in us, can really perform it. Third, the children of missionaries talk disrespectfully about the nationals and often offend them. Fourth, the missionaries don't judge the relative value of things and spend too much time in "hobbies." Fifth, the missionaries seldom, or never, take part in the social life of the people. Sixth, in spite of the tremendous amount of love they profess for us, their children are not sent either to the public school, or even to the evangelical school so they can learn our culture.[1]

Mr. Isais continues in the story, meetings should be held between the missionaries and nationals until they understand each other, and the problems can be ironed out. They are seeking to say to the missionary, that in a foreign culture it is not *what* is done that is so important but *how* it is done. The cup of water given in the right spirit is more important than the digging of a new well—in the wrong spirit.

The new missionary or the visitor to the mission field will be called upon to answer some of these questions. There again, the manner of his speech will be as important as the message he speaks.

Missionaries have heard all of these criticisms and a hundred more. Fortunately, there are nationals who love and appreciate the missionaries. I can still hear Deacon Chon at the Baptist Hospital in Pusan, Korea, praying, "O Lord, send us a thousand more like the halmoni." He was speaking of Miss Lucy Wright, who was retiring after forty-two years in China and Korea.

A young Burmese girl in New York said recently to a religious group, "You have heard it said from this platform that one religion is as good as another. If you had lived in my country, you would not say that. I have seen what years of religious superstition, fear, and indifference have done. We need the truth. We need missionaries who will present the uplift of Christianity. My country needs Christ."

We are forced to conclude that mission work has been a resounding success in spite of the many shortcomings. The "sharp contentions" of Paul and Barnabas have continued to plague missionaries, but still an effective ministry is continued. As the national churches develop, more missionaries will be needed. More specialists are needed, especially in the field of agriculture. Laymen are needed, even for short-term projects, where their skill can be shared with the national. Most national believers are still standing with the Macedonian saying, "Come over and help us."

Needed but not wanted was the descriptive phrase

of D. T. Niles. Could it be that this is the national's way of asking for a new *kind* of missionary?

Dr. Jonathan Chao, vice-president of the China Graduate School of Theology, writes in a letter:

In this post-missionary era, when most former mission fields have produced their own local, and sometimes indigenous churches, shouldn't the missionary and the mission executives conduct self-evaluations by consulting national leaders? Shouldn't the missionary enterprises be evaluated by the local national church, in addition to one-sided evaluation and recommendations by mission board representatives? If missions are to maintain one-way traffic in terms of decision-making, ignoring the leadership of the third world, then the non-Christian, or the anti-Christian (sometimes Communists) of the nations are right when they call missionary endeavors cultural imperialism of the West, particularly of America.[2]

Dr. Chao may draw some unwarranted conclusions, but still his is a voice to be heard. The national is saying that we need missionaries who will serve alongside us— not over us. The day of the great white father bestowing his beneficent blessings upon the children is gone. A new breed of missionary is being called for by the national church. This missionary would be one who recognizes that the Holy Spirit can work in and through a national as well as a missionary. To support the idea that the missionary must always be the leader is to insult the national.

We have noted ways to act to keep from insulting our national brethren. In the Orient, it is nice manners to give or receive most everything with two hands. In Bangladesh, use only your right hand, since the left hand is considered eternally unclean. The Japanese, with his abhorrence for touching a stranger, would prefer a bow rather than a handshake. To point your foot at a Thai is to insult him, and the list grows from country to country. However, perhaps the greatest insult we can give is when we fail to recognize the potential of the national. He can, and will, be used of the Holy Spirit.

I talked one day to a missionary administrator of a hospital. He said, "We would like to turn over the hospital to them (the nationals) but they are not ready." This particular group has been operating the hospital for over seventy-five years. They had some very capable leadership, but in the eyes of the veteran missionary they were still little children that needed his guiding hand.

The truth is, this has been the feeling of many missionaries. We hang on to the power, the finances, the top position until a crisis threatens, and then we are forced to turn it over to a group who is usually ill-prepared to operate it. How much better it would be to begin training leaders to take over the institutions with a definite goal in mind. Why wait until we are forced to do it? There is a rupture of fellowship then that can take years to heal.

[1] Juan Isais, *The Other Side of the Coin* (Grand Rapids: W. B. Eerdmans, Publisher, 1966), p. 51.
[2] Dr. Jonathan Chao, *Christianity Today,* January 19, 1973, p. 18.

Reflection #5

We had met in a small chapel to hear this missionary. Dr. H. Ranier had spent some twenty-seven years in India, Burma, and Tibet. We were only a small group of eight or ten, so Dr. Ranier spoke softly, but vibrantly. In his eyes was the light of God and he seemed as if possessed by the Spirit of the God he knew so well.

He and his wife had gone to India as a young missionary doctor and nurse. For years they labored in helping to relieve the pain of the sufferers. For the last four years, until 1961, he had been working near Tibet with the refugees that escaped from the Chinese Communists. They were seeking to make their way to India, or anywhere to escape the enemy.

Many were horribly diseased and Dr. Ranier tried to minister to as many cases as he could. Some were won to the Christian faith. Among these, were four lamas who were converted and became witnesses of their new faith. Twice, Dr. Ranier was captured by the Communists. Once he escaped and once he was permitted to escape (the Communists thought he would die in the frozen wilderness). Many times during an operation they would announce an evacuation, however, Dr. Ranier and his patient would have to stay and often narrowly missed being captured. He was utterly dedicated to this task. Soon he told us why.

In the dark war days of the early forties, the disastrous typhus fever struck the northern part of India. Dr. Ranier ministered to people day and night with his faithful wife by his side. Thousands died. Soon his wife was stricken. All the medicine he possessed was of no avail and amid the sorrowing of fellow sufferers she slipped into eternity. Dr. Ranier and his fourteen-year-old son had to take her some twenty-two miles to a cemetery that would permit a foreigner to be buried there. It was late in the afternoon when they returned, numb with grief, seemingly friendless, and still amid strangers in a pagan land. From a distance they saw smoke and when they arrived at home their house was on fire and their furnishings were charred ruins. The authorities said any foreigner who died with the disease would have to have everything burned to prevent the spread of the typhus.

Brokenhearted, his wife dead, his house burned, his books, medical equipment, and medicine all destroyed, the doctor sat on a log in front of his house and wept. It was then that his fourteen-year-old son came, put his arm around his weeping father, and said, "Don't cry Dad, you still have Jesus and me." Two weeks later his son died. Now he only had Jesus. Just the doctor and Jesus in a land of unbelief, sickness, sin, and death. In a lonely cemetery in the backward ramparts of India, were the lonely graves of a faithful wife and a fourteen-year-old son, soldiers of the cross, who had been faithful unto death.

Dr. Ranier reasoned with himself. Should he return to Australia, his home, and to his friends? Back there would be comfort, friendship, and freedom. He looked north toward Tibet—a land where there was not a single church. A land closed to the gospel. A land where his beloved Savior was completely unknown.

He looked toward the east. Here lay the two people he had loved most on the earth. They had not shrunk back. They went to the grave with the battle flag of Christianity still clutched in hands that had not grown weary in well-doing.

The doctor packed his few small possessions and turned north toward Tibet. God has marvelously used his talent there to heal the sick and to tell the ageless story of hope, heaven, and inward peace.

Most of us were weeping unashamedly when the Australian missionary had finished. The little chapel had been transformed into a majestic cathedral and the power of the Holy Spirit could be felt. Most of his hearers were missionaries in Korea, called out to make the Savior known in this pagan land. However, I had some serious doubt as to whether or not that Dr. Ranier and I could be called "missionaries" in the same sense.

5.
What Makes a Good Missionary?

The sign in the church hallway said, "Every person in the world is a missionary . . . or he needs one." There is a sense in which every Christian is a witness, but most assuredly, not every man is to be a home or foreign missionary. Every person should bear a witness and be a missionary in his home community. However, the evangelization of the greater community of mankind calls for a special type of person. There are missionaries and there are good missionaries. What is the difference?

In Acts 13:2, the Holy Spirit said, "Set apart for me Barnabas and Saul for the work to which I have called them" (RSV). Here God not only directed the lives of the individuals involved but also brought the missionary call to the door of the church. God works in and through his church. The church was to be a part of the mission endeavor. Men were to be set apart for this cause. Neither the church nor the men would doubt that God had called.

For some, this call may be highly dramatic with tremendous upheaval in their lives. For most men and women it comes with a quiet conviction and assurance that the Lord wants them there.

Robert Hastings, in an editorial in the *Illinois Baptist*, questions the use of the term "surrender" when a person enters the ministry or accepts a post of duty in Christian work. He sees doing God's will as a great victory and hesitates to connect it with a word which means defeat. Whatever else it is, the call is that which keeps a man on the field when almost everything else says leave. The Lord does call, move, motivate, and empower people for special ministries. Some are called to a definite place or country, others feel called to serve where they may be needed most. The career or professional missionary goes, intending to remain in that country, or at least in overseas services, until the Lord leads him to another field of service.

The missionary must remain as open to the further leadership of God as the pastor or denominational worker. He needs to be sure that he is open to the leadership of the Holy Spirit and not bound by just rules of the board that sent him out. It is difficult to say that a foreign missionary has a "lifetime" call to a certain field. This is seldom said of the pastor, or seminary professor, or denominational worker. Geographical distance hardly changes a man's openness to the Lord's leadership.

Many missionaries go to a country and work forty years and wish they had another forty to give. This is the norm for the career missionary, but if the Lord closes the door, or if the nationals are able to do all the work, then he should feel free to move to another field or return to a place of service in the homeland. Merely because a person knows the language and culture does not constitute a lifetime call. On that basis, he could have served effectively in his homeland, for there he knew the language and culture from the beginning.

The importance of the call should never be underestimated. It is this that gives one the "partnership-with-God" feeling and the joy of doing God's will. A missionary comes to the field, learns the language, makes many friends, and has many contacts with the nationals. He is a shrewd businessman and sees the opportunity to make a fortune. The real estate market is wide open, or he could deal in diamonds, furs, or pearls. Banks are paying 15 to 20 percent interest on investments, and as a "citizen" of both worlds he could have an "inside" into this market. He could be a millionaire in ten or fifteen years . . . but then he realizes he owes allegiance to the Lord. His loyalty is to his Master and he is willing to forsake the treasures of Egypt for the privilege of knowing Christ. The temptation is there, but so is a commitment to Christ.

His parents grow old. Heartrending letters cross the ocean. His own children grow up and return to the United States for college. Family pressure is always strong to return home "for you are needed here." He looks, but then remembers that God has the higher priority. Perhaps facing persecution, suffering anguish, braving danger, he comes to realize that the safest place is where God wants him to be, be it in Lebanon, Uganda, or Chile. As Jeremiah of old, the Word of God

burns in his bones. His call is not based on his acceptance by the nationals, or the surrounding circumstances, but on a fixed allegiance to the Lord Christ.

Relationships

How important this is throughout life. It is vital that
the missionary maintain a growing relationship with
the Lord. Prayer and Bible study are neglected at the
peril of one's own spiritual health. Cease to pray and
you start to play at being a servant of the Lord. The
connection with the power source is to remain open,
giving the missionary a holy enthusiasm for serving
the Lord. This can't be emphasized too much. It is
absolutely vital to an effective work. Be astray here
and the other relationships will sour. Out of step with
the Lord will hardly help your marching with the
Lord's people.

How often we are brought to realize that our problems are really spiritual, when we blame something
else. We make excuses, we invent activities, we become
sensitive and self-possessive about our work, when all
the time we know that things are not right with the
Lord. We harbor a grudge, have ill feelings toward
someone else, and know this will have to be confessed
and forsaken before other relationships will be right.
Troublesome areas can usually be traced to a lack of
spiritual insight, or the lack of the fruits of the Spirit
in our lives. Dr. Mary Stone of China used to say, "Each
day I look first into the face of Jesus, and then the
face of sick Chinese look beautiful." She had learned
to draw strength from that union with Christ. Jesus

said, "I am the vine, you are the branches" (John 15:5, RSV). There must be a vital growing union here or no fruit can be produced. Melinda Rankin, of Mexico, declared that the word *pessimism* has no place in the Christian's vocabulary. Just another way of saying, "Rejoice, for I have overcome the world" (see John 16:33).

Dr. Baker James Cauthen, executive secretary of the Foreign Mission Board, had this in mind when he told some newly appointed missionaries:

You may be a superman, but I doubt it. My guess is that you are "just folks," like the rest of us. You are people in whom the Spirit of God is at work. You have your high moments and your low moments. You will go to your task realizing that the enemy of mankind will do all he can to make you grow discouraged. If he has his way, you will not stay. He will make you give up if he can, because you are invading his domain. You are on territory that he doesn't want you to occupy. Many testings await you, and you will be glad the Bible says, "Hope in God." [1]

The testings, hardships, privations, and separation from loved ones can be met with the strength we draw from the Vine. He will give the strength for the crisis when the crisis comes; not before. He will open the door to escape when the temptation is there, though you cannot see it now. "Thanks be unto God who gives us the victory" (1 Cor. 15:57, RSV), though you may not yet be in the arena. There is no other relationship for the producing of grapes as that between the Vine and the branches. "My help cometh from the Lord" (Ps. 121:2) must be the missionary's motto. The day by day routine, the grinding cycle of poverty and the heavy schedule of activities will wear away at the missionary unless he is determined to maintain a growing spiritual union with Christ.

The second important relationship is with the national. His language and culture should be a main concern of the missionary in the early years. The language becomes a tool to the missionary, it is a means of doing his work. If he has only a halfhearted smattering of it, then it will be reflected in his work. The indictment by the Guatemalan chief who said, "If your God is so great, why doesn't he speak my language?" is serious. Communication is vital. The early years of a missionary's career must be consumed in language study.

Understanding the culture of the national is also necessary. Someone has observed that it is probably better that it takes the missionary several years to be able to express himself adequately. During that time he can also learn the culture and know what *not* to say. There have been missionaries who knew the language but still had difficulty in communicating with the people. It is true that love, as well as music, is a universal language. It speaks to hearts everywhere, under every condition, and in a measure that will be long remembered. Paul knew this to be true and stated in 1 Corinthians 13, "If I speak in the tongues of men and of angels, but have not love, I am a noisy gong or a clanging cymbal" (v. 2, RSV). The greatest missionaries are those with a deep abiding love for the culture and the people.

Proving the "sincerity of your love" is the task for

the man overseas or he becomes a spiritual cripple. "If you love me, lean on me," said the elderly Chinese to the weary missionary. Perhaps the national could preface many of his requests with, "If you love me." Christ spent a lot of time after the resurrection talking with Peter. The burden of that conversation was not the church, or Peter's denial, or even Peter's attitude toward the Gentiles. It had to do with love. "Lovest thou me" had to be settled before he could preach to Jew or Gentile. The missionary had served more than thirty years in India, and just before retirement confessed, "I've hated them, I've hated them . . . all these years I've been here, I've hated them." What a vessel to bear the love of God to a lost people!

The national may be impressed by your knowledge and interested in your technology, but he will only be moved by love. Note how often Paul spoke of love to the various people scattered across Asia Minor. It has been said that you can go 18,000 miles, but it is the last eighteen inches that really count. On the field the "touch" ministry is not optional, it's mandatory.

Sometimes it is easier to forsake all people rather than forsake all "things." We have grown accustomed to our possessions and we take our culture with us. "Is there anything the American does not have?" asked one national of another. They had just unloaded his household goods. There were three radios, a record player, a tape recorder, a typewriter, and a calculator. The national had previously lived in a rural community where they shared one radio. The speakers were located in various sections of the village and all the people were "blessed" with the radio for about twelve hours each day.

Whether we agree with it or not, in the eyes of the nationals the missionary is usually considered rich. In some countries he may have to take a four-year supply of shoes and other clothing. Household items cannot be purchased locally, so he brings them. He desires that his children grow up surrounded by familiar things. When a villager is sick, the missionary may have the only automobile in the area. When there is disaster, flood or fire, he may be the only one in touch with the outside world. The fact that he possesses all the "things" places a heavy burden on him. Some missionaries withdraw behind their possessions. Others share or give away everything to the extent that they need help themselves. Somewhere there is a balance, and the missionary will have to find it and live with it.

Dr. John Abernathy, longtime missionary to China and Korea, had a favorite word to new missionaries. "You'll just have to learn to cope with it." The fact that some of us ran out of "cope" quite soon did not lessen the meaning of his message. When the current is only 220 volts and all your appliances are 110, your transformer was stolen last night, or your car is broken down and you have four churches to visit, then cope. "My friend, you'll just have to cope with it."

Few missionaries take the vow of poverty when they depart for the field. The national does not expect it. He knows America is an affluent nation and could hardly expect the American to be otherwise. He doesn't resent the missionary's possessions, but he can be made to resent the American's attitude toward those possessions.

One missionary received a new briefcase for Christmas. The next day he called in his language teacher and there before his eyes, transferred all the material from the old briefcase to the new one. Then with a holy look of benevolence gave the old one to his language teacher. Five years later the teacher was still raving about the total lack of love and respect in the missionary. Benevolence 12, Attitude 0. Only the missionary was good enough for the new briefcase. The manner of giving can be a lot more important than the gift.

The American overseas needs to watch out for what missionary Gordon Saltau called the "downward slant." It is that built-in superiority complex we take with us. We are college-trained, seminary-educated, widely traveled, and cosmopolitan in outlook. The United States is the greatest, our Olympic teams are the finest, and our way of life is the most desirable. We become the living epitome of the joke in such poor taste that has the missionary saying, "Get out of my way you idiot, don't you know I'm over here to help you."

This is often manifested in the old paternalistic spirit. "My Chinese," or my "beloved African," meaning a protecting, preserving attitude. We use the ethnic slant in such a way that implies superiority and more ability in everything. Increasingly nationalism is attacking us at this very point. Ethnic slurs, racial prejudices, and the downward slant had best be buried in an unlamented grave. In the cartoon, "The Wizard of Id," a decree was made that no more ethnic jokes were to be told. Then Rodney says, "That doesn't stand a China-man's chance of being enforced." Rodney, like the overseas visitor, has his culture, too.

The missionary must watch his language. In many countries there are levels of speech to superiors, equals, or to children that must be observed. It is grossly impo-lite for missionaries to speak English in the presence of a national, when the national does not understand. This can create ill feelings and much misunderstand-ing. The matter of "face" is most important. A public rebuke is hard for the national to accept when adminis-tered by a foreigner. It reflects on him, his ancestors, even his nation. Never back a man in a corner where he has no way to save face. Enemies can be made that will impair mission work for years. Moreover, the national does not want the guest of his country to lose face. Their culture calls for a "face-saving" even in the face of expediency.

One missionary helped a church with some building funds. Before they began construction, a deacon died, and the pastor used the money for funeral expenses. The missionary then berated the nationals for this misappropriation of funds. The poor pastor was horri-fied. What kind of a callous person would have a friend die and not have a big funeral in his honor. Indeed, the missionary was coldhearted and had no love for the culture, the people, or for the "face" of the church, as the pastor saw it.

In speaking, especially in public, the missionary must

be careful in using humor. The nationals might laugh when one of their own pastors joke about their customs or their government, but it would scarcely be funny coming from a foreigner. One missionary, thinking he was teasing the pastor, actually caused the poor fellow to lose much face before the congregation. I recall trying to inject a humorous point in a sermon in Korean. It consisted mainly of how people hear one message, then another, so they hardly know what to believe. The well-worn story of the farmer who called his pigs by yodeling was told. Later he had a throat operation, and being unable to yodel, would call his pigs to eat by knocking on a tree. This worked fine until a flock of woodpeckers got into his field and then the pigs ran themselves to death. Inwardly I congratulated myself on being able to use such a good illustration in the language. Later while having lunch with the pastor, he commented on the farmer's story and then, sucking air through his teeth, said, "Oh, I was so sorry to hear he had the throat operation." Most often they will miss the humor and make the wrong application. I've seen a congregation rock with laughter over some insignificant thing their pastor would tell that would not be humorous at all to an outsider. As in all languages, much of the humor is a play on words, or some outlandish pronunciation.

A blustery Western cattleman, sharing his Christian testimony to a congregation in a foreign land, demanded that the interpreter say exactly what he said, "nothing more, nothing less." The intimidated interpreter agreed. The rancher, upon being introduced, rushed to the pulpit and said, "Well, here I am, an hour late and a dollar short." The interpreter hesitated only a moment and said, "The honored gentleman says he has arrived. However, he arrived one hour late, and the reason he was late was that he lacked a dollar having enough to pay his fare."

What makes a good missionary? It is the same qualities that will make a good pastor, or a good professor, or a good businessman. It is a down-to-earth openness that makes a man willing to confess his weaknesses and big enough to overcome them. Dependability and willingness are great pillars that hold up the missionary image. Approachability and integrity will cause a man to be long-remembered on the mission field. When all of these qualities are coupled with a deep spiritual commitment and an abiding love dwelling in the Lord, then you have a person who will be a good missionary at home or abroad.

[1] Baker James Cauthen, *Beyond Call* (Nashville: Broadman Press, 1973), p. 58.

Reflection #6

She walked, bent forward, as is the manner of elderly women, even though she was probably under forty years of age. A faded apron covered part of a faded dress. On her arm was a big basket partially filled with fruit that she was selling. Since early morning she had walked the dirty streets of Manila, wearily approaching stranger after stranger trying to eke out enough to feed her family. She had long ceased to be interested in her appearance, and the wind played havoc with her hair. Wrinkles and lines adorned the bronze face and a worried look revealed much of her present poverty. Gnarled hands sought to keep flies away from the bananas in the bamboo basket, but the effort was hardly enough to discourage the flies. Long ago she had given in to the flies, just as she accepted the inevitable hunger of her people. Her eyes moved back and forth over the few people that rushed by, somehow knowing they would buy nothing. Most could afford the cheap meal at the restaurant. Only those who could afford nothing better would buy her bananas.

Now and then she cried out, 'sa-geen, sa-geens for sale,' in a loud voice. The day was far spent and her energy had been expended with it. She still had a long walk ahead of her. There would be no money for bus fare. Whatever else you might say, at least she had tried.

Her kind was not unknown in the city, for there are many who look just as worn and work just as hard. I passed her by with little more than a curious look. It was only when I saw the child that I began to notice with interest.

Obviously, there was no one with whom she could leave the little girl, who looked to be about five years old. The tot trailed her mother by about twenty feet, stopping occasionally to invest some childish interest in some fascination. Her dress matched the mothers in fadedness, and an untied ribbon hung down from the jet black hair. All day long she had followed the steps of her mother—stopping when she stopped, running sometimes to keep up. While my five-year-old played games in a clean kindergarten, this one received her education along the gutted sidewalks of the city. She was exhausted now. She would walk a few steps, and then lean against the building, moving only when her mother motioned with her hand.

All of this panorama of twisted humanity happened in an instant. I sat in the car waiting for a traffic light to change and observed this drama of daily survival. The honking of the car behind me moved me from the trance and I had to drive on—probably never to see the mother and the tired little girl anymore. And yet, I've seen them a hundred times since that moment. I see them when I sit down to a table burdened with food. Sometimes the shrill cry of "sa-geen, sa-geen" cuts through the loneliness of a quiet evening. I see my happy little girl dressed in Sunday's finery, and in the background another little girl stands looking at her mother, waiting for a signal that would tell her to move along.

If only I could have done something. For less than fifty cents I could have bought every banana in that basket. Maybe just a smile, and pat the little girl on the head . . . just say something, or do something that would convey a message to restore her faith in humanity and let the little girl know that someone cares. Instead, I just moved on. I let the honking horn of a rushing world move me . . . not the drama of real life.

6.
When Is Mission Work Actually Being Done?

The American soldier returned to his homeland and reported that there were many churches in Korea but no missionaries. "I was there for thirteen months and never saw a missionary." In reality there were over one thousand two hundred missionaries there at the time and almost one hundred of them were Southern Baptist. The missionaries were not often in military camps or the tourist belt, so the young soldier just assumed none were there.

It is hardly possible to visit a country for only a few days and see all the mission work. It helps to know what to look for. Statistics and pretty maps cannot tell the full story. In 1812, Adoniram Judson went to Burma. He witnessed there for six years before he had his first convert. He spent many hours translating the Bible into Burmese. In all of his ministry there, part of which was spent in jail, he only had a few hundred converts. Suppose someone had visited him after he had been there for only a few years. Could they possibly have seen the value of a Bible in a native dialect? Would they have been able to envision the 250,000 Baptists that would someday be there?

Most of us have a preconceived idea of what mission work really is. For some it may be the old pith-helmeted safari winding along the jungle streams, or the fiery missionary preaching in the crowded market-place, or the kindly doctor treating a neglected case of beriberi. Some are able to see the microphone, the airplane, the tractor, even the computer being used. The day-by-day toil, the vast number of disappointments, the quiet walk with God, and the bitter hours of loneliness are seldom noticed.

According to the *Evangelical Mission Quarterly* some comparative figures can be enlightening. In Africa in 1900, there were twenty-eight non-Christians for every Christian. In Asia the ratio was seventy-five to one. Seventy-five years later it was twenty-two non-Christians to every Christian in Asia and two and five tenths to one in Africa. Meanwhile, we have 95 percent of the forty thousand Protestant missionaries working with 17 percent of the world's people. This means that the vast Hindu, Muslim, and Chinese population, constituting 83 percent of the world's population, has only 5 percent of the missionaries. It would take 212,000 more missionaries to evangelize the 83 percent in the same proportion that we are working with the 17 percent.

These figures reveal that a lot of mission work is being done and the results are good. In all of the eighty-two countries combined, Southern Baptists report 896,000 baptized members. Brazil, our largest field, has 371,729, followed by Nigeria with 122,000. India reports only 188 members in churches working with

Southern Baptist missionaries and Gaza has only forty-four. Yet, when the fields are examined, much more is being done than can be reported. Some fields are productive and blossom like Korea, where there are more than two million evangelicals. Across the strait is Japan where only one in a hundred is a Christian. Thailand, after twenty-five years of mission work by Baptists, has sixty-four missionaries, eighteen churches, and 1,414 baptized members. The missionaries there labor long hours, but the results are few. Thus, if we are number conscious, we may be in for some disillusionment. We may become like the pastor who kneeled before the Sunday School register board and prayed.

O God of numbers on the wall,
Give me 1,700 or none at all.
Lest I, like the apostle Paul,
Be let down o'er the city wall.

However, we do have to have some criteria, some standard of measurement after years of missionary service in order to measure the results. Someone was conscious of numbers in the Bible. Jesus fed the five thousand. There were three thousand saved at Pentecost, and a great host which no man could number was seen in a vision. Church growth missiologists, under the leadership of Dr. Donald McGavran, have devised ways and means of studying a mission field to determine its productiveness. Responsive areas, people movements toward receiving the gospel are given wide attention. Hard and stony areas where the gospel seed will not produce much are staffed only with a small force, while the main concentration of personnel would be at the responsive places. Largely, this has been done as evidenced by the small number of missionaries in Muslim and Hindu areas. Yet the "fields are white unto harvest," and the field is the world. Starving people are in need of the Water of life every place. The visitor to the mission field needs an awareness of these growth factors. His assessment of the field, with these facts in mind, will be more accurate.

Very often what a visitor sees and what he thinks he sees may be poles apart. One layman returned to his church and said, "Sometimes I wonder about our missionaries out there. One day while driving in the city, we came to a busy intersection. A blind beggar, led by a little girl, approached the car. The missionary ignored them and their outstretched hands until the light changed and then we moved on. They just don't love the people as they should," This is what he saw; this is what influenced him. This is one thing he reported back home.

What he did not see was the organization which exploits the blind and the lame. They send them into dangerous intersections to beg, giving them very little, and they pocket the rest. One "blind institute" in the Philippines was lending money at an exorbitant interest rate and ultimately had a lawsuit brought against it. Lame and blind children have been exploited in many Oriental countries by cruel masters. Some countries have had people to maim a child deliberately in order to use him as a begging object. In some areas to give alms to beggars is to encourage this nefarious activity. There are ways to give and help these people but open handouts may not be the best way. The tragedy was that the layman overlooked perhaps years of faithful mission work to report this. Some missionaries have just adopted a policy of giving a little to each of them. If it's abused or misused, then it's a small price to pay in view of being able to truly help one now and then.

"The missionary has a maid, a cook, and a gardner," cried the visitor, "meanwhile he goes to an air-conditioned office and piddles around with some old books." True, true, about the maid and the cook. Most missionaries will have at least one where it can be afforded. In some countries they are paid twenty-five dollars to fifty dollars per month, and this is more than nationals will be paying for the same type of help. Sometimes it is just an act of charity. The girls especially, are practically kicked out of their homes. They can starve, become prostitutes, or a few can be employed with dignity in a missionary home. Often the missionary's wife will have several jobs to do, plus an unusual amount of company. A thirty dollar a month maid may release a missionary for a full-time job. As for piddling around in the office, someone has to write those Sunday School lessons, tracts, gospel books, and other literature. Television and radio programs must be planned. Most missions need a treasurer, business manager, and office personnel. Also, if a missionary is teaching a class each day, it will take a lot of studying.

This is not written to justify lazy missionaries. Anytime you get 2,700 people working on a project, some will be akin to Rip Van Winkle. A person may be lazy upon coming to the mission field, but it is hard to remain that way. Dozens of jobs have to be left undone because everyone is busy. The call to go, give, teach, and reach out a helping hand is always with you.

Laziness is not as much a problem as is majoring on the minors. We can get so wrapped up in "programs" that provide a lot of diversion and activity but add little toward our goal. The peripheral ministry captures the attention and the weightier matters are left undone. We plead with the voice of Jacob and work with hands of Esau. The Isaacs may be deceived, but the mess of pottage is hardly satisfying. The missionary would do well to begin the day by praying that he would be delivered from a ministry of trivialities.

It's true that the ministry of the missionary is like that of the salesman. It's hard to make many sales sitting at a desk. Someone, perhaps Parkinson, said that the amount of work is in diverse proportion to the time spent at a desk. Certainly this could be true of the mission field. Just let a man get a desk, an office, and soon he is burdened down with administrative work. Then, too, this work has a beguiling effect in that we come to believe the office work must be done even if other things have to wait. The office can mean the death of evangelistic fire in the missionary unless he divides his time so that some time will be spent witnessing in the marketplace.

It was great advice that the Home Mission Board evangelist gave to his fellow workers when he admonished them to let their shirt pocket be their office. If you outgrow that, use a briefcase, and from that go to the trunk of your car. An office demands office hours, and office hours will keep you off the field and this will cripple your work. Somewhere there is a balance to be struck that will ensure the needed office work and place a major emphasis on evangelism. This I believe the layman would like to see, and deserves to see, when he visits the mission field.

Another hard-to-see fact of mission work is the bearing of the missionary. The fact that he left his homeland, his parents, and an easier life to come here and live, speaks of love. His presence gives a great testimony to his concern. Just be sure the words and conduct do not distract from that witness.

One summer, our high school daughter was permitted to work as an aide in the Baptist Hospital in Pusan, Korea. A lady come in for the birth of her child. She had previously given birth to six daughters and her husband had practically demanded she have a boy. When the husband came to the hospital, his wife told him it "was only a girl." Without saying a word, he stormed out of the hospital. The wife turned her face into the pillow and wept. My wife asked our daughter what she did. "I didn't know what to do," she said, "so I just put my head on the pillow and wept with her." I doubt if all the work she did that summer would equal that measure of love and concern. There are times when all of us have that helpless feeling, and in the face of such frustrations all we can do is weep with them.

The missionary must remember at all times that he is a guest in the country and remains there only by the permission of the government. His relationship to the government is of great importance. Visas, work permits, alien registration certificates, drivers licenses, and all the other requirements must be honored by the missionary. Many countries are under martial law or the rule of the military. There are often conflicts over particular issues and it takes a double measure of patience and self-control. Customs examiners, city officials, and petty military rulers will exert their authority, exhaust your patience, and demand every ounce of grace you have. Rudyard Kipling had this in mind when he wrote the epitaph, "Here lies a fool who tried to hustle the east." You may know a better way, a quicker way, and a cheaper way, but it is not the national's way.

Kindness and courtesy can pay huge dividends in these offices. Leave your calling card, express a word of appreciation, invite them into your home—this type of conduct will bring many blessings and is like applying oil on squeaking machinery.

In one Oriental city the missionaries had the reputation for being honest. When you came in via ship or plane, the customs officials would seldom open your baggage if they knew you were a missionary. Confidence such as that must not be abused. It is a way of bearing a witness and winning friends for Christianity. This holds true for your relationship with schools, barrio officials, and anyone else you contact. The witness of the missionary begins when he steps ashore.

A policeman was admitted to a missionary hospital. The kindness, love, and concern did not go unnoticed.

He accepted Christ and declared his intentions of returning to his village and building a church there. He exclaimed how much his poor village needed the helpful spirit of the Christian people.

A missionary received his receipt and the young clerk said, "Thank you, Father." Immediately he launched a tirade against being called father, specifically, and the Roman church, generally. Other workers listened to what he was saying. The young secretary was embarrassed, and it caused her to lose face before her fellow workers. She never called another missionary "Father," and it is doubtful if she ever forgave the missionary for embarrassing her in public.

Many people in Manila have accepted Christ because one missionary has shown an interest in public officials. He inquires about their family or their hometown. He always knows someone that they know and strikes a friendly conversation. He has a positive, nonthreatening way of presenting the gospel and the results are amazing. You would hardly know the extent of his ministry by merely reading his job description. It has been noted that the Christian is to be like a sponge, absorbing all the hate, envy, and jealously around him, and then transforming that into love and kindness and returning it to the community.

Another ministry that may be difficult to see is the ministry of intercessory prayer. Prayer is the most powerful weapon the missionary can use. It will break down barriers, mend broken spirits, heal the wounded hearts, and move the minds of men. The nine children of Reverend and Mrs. John Scudder of India have all given their lives to missionary service in that land. This one family has given a total of 530 years of continuous missionary service to the people of India. Mr. Scudder indicates that the children were literally prayed into the kingdom by their mother. She was accustomed to praying all day for each child on his birthday. Mrs. Scudder had a vital impact on India, but this intercessory praying may have been the most important thing she did.

Between Japan and Korea is the island of Ullung Do. Thanks to a short medical work and some immigration, there are now fifteen Baptist churches on the small island. Several years ago a typhoon struck the island, crippling the fishing industry. A Baptist deacon in Chu Shan lost his boat and with it went the total income of the church there. Most of the male church members worked on the boat and now they were destitute. Southern Baptists made possible eighty dollars in relief money to help replace the boat. The pastor wrote me the letter of appreciation and said, "As Daniel turned toward Jerusalem and prayed, we hope that each day you will turn toward our island and pray." However Baptists looked upon the relief money, he saw it as an answer to prayer.

The mighty apostle Paul constantly exhorted churches to pray for him or for his fellow workers. He catalogued all his suffering, shipwrecks, being whipped, and then said on top of all that, that his concern was for the churches. He knew and he was concerned. The more awareness we have of our national co-workers, the more we will pray for them. Pastor

Kang was not one of my favorite pastors until one day he told me of leaving North Korea and coming south, skirting the fighting that was taking place in the summer of 1950. He and his family were so hungry they ate the bark of trees before the ordeal was over. Somehow after knowing this, and how he had suffered at the hands of the Communists, I found it a joy to pray for him.

The missionaries presence, suffering when they suffer, rejoicing when they rejoice, is a real evidence of concern and will touch the heart of the national. One missionary wife in Japan helped her national neighbor during a long illness. The missionary would drop in a few minutes each day to clean the room, or bring her a bowl of soup, or perform some small task. The missionary is dead today, but this lady has now accepted Christ as her Lord and says it was this love that opened her heart to the Christian message.

Mission work is being done when it involves training the national. The ministry of the missionary can be multiplied by well trained national workers. Jesus spent so much of his earthly ministry training and teaching the twelve. Paul's warmest epistles are those to his young helpers in the ministry. He commanded Timothy, "The same commit thou to faithful men, who shall be able to teach others also" (2 Tim. 2:2). Training, teaching, equipping national workers is an essential part of a continuing ministry. Seminaries, Bible schools, and good literature are vital needs and should play a large role in the plans of any mission. The crowd would leave Jesus talking about the miracles, but it was the training of the twelve that would ensure the ongoing of the work.

It is good to use dedicated laypeople and pastors from the United States for overseas crusades. This usually involves a church, or churches, in a citywide effort to win the lost. However, would it not also be useful to use them once in awhile for conferences, seminars, and workshops related to training those who are believers? We have pastors who do not know how to pastor a flock, deacons that know little of the function of their office, and the same is true of church clerks, Sunday School workers, and church treasurers. Retired people could come and stay for a year or more teaching in such conferences.

Mission work is being done when the nationals are being related to Christ in a vital union that results in their being fruitful. This means an active church program in the teaching ministries. It means a stewardship development and a life-style that reflects their commitment. It means a desire to see others saved and an emphasis on missions in their community and to the outside world.

There are many para-church groups on the mission field today. They major on witnessing or some type of service. Among these missionaries you can detect a high degree of frustration, in that they realize their work will cease when they leave. If everything is dependent on the outside missionary, you have a weak mission work. The report of 10,000 tracts distributed, 150 students witnessed to, and meals served to 20,000 people is great. But what will the results be next year?

If the work is not within the framework of the local churches, its lasting value may be questioned. Making disciples and having them functioning in a local New Testament church pattern, which has the desire to reach out and begin other churches, is the ideal. For this we must strive.

Reflection #7

"Manners," so Emily Post is credited with saying, "are a sensitive awareness of the feelings of others. If you have that awareness, you have good manners, no matter what fork you use." The works of Miss Post, and I say this to my detriment, have seldom claimed a major portion of my time. However, the above quotation reveals a depth of wisdom that causes me to hunger for more. I realize now that I have been in the presence of some of the foremost mannerists in the world. They may not know a dinner fork from a salad fork, but they fulfill the spirit of etiquette. If considering the needs of others is the criteria, they not only heaped coals of fire on my head, they emptied the coal bin. It makes you feel like a hippopotamus amidst a field of graceful swan, or a GI boot in a ladies' shoe store. An example please.

The four of us gathered around the table, seated on the floor. The fishing family was poor, and I knew we were taking a good share of their rations. I glanced stealthily at my watch. It was some two hours past my regular breakfast hour, but then this was no regular breakfast. The family of six had been up long before daylight preparing the food.

The mother came in with a gray rag and again scrubbed the table. Soon she began placing the soy sauce, bean curd, bean sprouts, and assorted "panchan" near the center of the table. Next came the hot soup and the covered bowls of rice. Though she had correctly placed everything on the table, she again touched almost every dish as she readjusted the space allocation.

Down near the coldest part of the room (the warmest area

was occupied by the foreigner), sat the fisherman. His arms were crossed and his hands entwined in the ample sleeves of his toga. He was blessed with humility but still managed to give the appearance of a patriarch on his throne. The mother took the gray rag and again wiped an imaginary spot from the top of my rice bowl. Then with a culinary flourish, worthy of a Parisian chef, she indicated to the fisherman that breakfast was ready. "Kito hapsita," was his only acknowledgment.

After the prayer, the fisherman apologized for having so little to set before such distinguished guests, and begged that we eat much. The mother had retreated, but remained smiling and alert so as to anticipate our every need. She knelt near the small kitchen door as if to preside over the activities of both areas. With averted eyes she still managed an "amen" to the prayer and also beseeched us to eat much. Fish that had been broiled in a delicious manner was on the table, but the fisherman never touched it until the guest had finished. Conversation was scarce, but the clacking chopsticks wove a pattern of music familiar to every household.

During the meal, I moved, fidgeted, coiled, and uncoiled, but the fisherman never moved. I had cushions fore and aft; he sat on the barren, polished floor. Searing red pepper introduced me to a section of hades seldom encountered, but the matchless lady countered with some cool barley tea. Sweat broke out across a wrinkled brow and a fan materialized from the background. I attempted to straighten out a kinked leg and two people moved to make room. The fisherman arched an eyebrow and two sons scurried to do his bidding. Never in restaurants from San Francisco to Hong

Kong, had genuine service flowed in such a selfless manner.

Words of gratitude never seemed so inadequate. I tried to toss out verbal bouquets of roses but received arm loads of orchids in return. As the door slid open, I had three people to help me down the steps. Shoes were produced and slipper spoons guided my clumsy feet to the right shoes. Across the way the bronzed fisherman never looked down, and somehow stepped straight into his komoshins. We bowed, shook hands three or four times, and the whole family followed us to the gate. Again the family bowed, but the fisherman was to accompany us all the way to our boat.

Today, in a world where manners have given way to expediency, I just wanted to tip my hat to that wonderful fisherman's family on Ullung Do (Island). Their wonderful hospitality was only exceeded by their gracious manners, and just think, they never even heard of Emily!

7.

What the National Can Do That the Foreigner Cannot Do

While living in Taegu, Korea, we knew an independent Baptist missionary who became convicted over his life-style. The missionaries lived in large comfortable houses, while most nationals lived in small two-room houses with a lean-to for the kitchen. Many of these were made of mud blocks and had sliding paper doors. He decided to move out and live exactly as the poorer people in the community.

He rented a small mud block house in the outskirts of Pohang, and moved into it with his wife and two small children. The Korean women there would go to the well and draw a large bucket of water, place it on their heads, and gracefully walk back to their houses. The missionary's wife tried this. The bucket fell off her head bringing gales of laughter from the Koreans. Moreover, she was completely unable to wash her clothes in the running stream. She was so embarrassed that she refused to go back to the well, which meant that the man must go. Now the men in Korea work hard, but carrying water is strictly for the ladies. This man carrying water brought on renewed laughter and much ridicule. At night, the rural people, curious about foreigners, would creep to the paper door and punch small holes in it and watch them. Their being there was like a free sideshow for the nationals. They remained there for two nerve-racking weeks, moved back into the city, and shortly left the mission field altogether.

Now, I'm well aware that missionaries, worldwide, would be able to quote instances where they have lived like the nationals, with no trouble. Of course, we can all do this if we can choose the national. Thanks to the growing economy in Korea, the picture would be different today. However, in vast sections of Asia, Southeast Asia, the Middle East, and Africa, it is hazardous to attempt living without pure water, screened houses, sanitation, a refrigerator, and a balanced diet.

Had a Korean pastor or evangelist gone to the Pohang area to live, he would have encountered no difficulty. The national can live in his economy without calling attention to it. He is able to move freely among the people and converse with them in a language he learned while at his mother's knee. Even at his best, the missionary cannot do this. Also, for the rich Western missionary to try to live as the poorer of the nationals, when they know he has access to much better, is to make mockery of their life-style. This is no defense of the missionary living as a king among paupers. Most of us could and should do with far less. Neither do I believe we need to take the vow of poverty. We can seek to live simply, yet adequately, without flaunting our wealth before people whose income may be less than two hundred dollars per year.

The point is to observe the difficulty for the Westerner in this area and the ease which the national has in doing this. He is not hung up on guilt feelings about having a refrigerator. He does not try to do outlandish things to prove that he loves the people. His life-style is tailored to be as the people around him. It provokes no problems; it calls for no attention.

This has been a Western fly in the Oriental ointment for years. Many missions have made valiant effort to do something about it. It is embarrassing when the missionary's home is larger than the seminary dormitory, or the nicest building in the whole city is the missionary compound. The missionaries and the Christian nationals are concerned about it and are seeking ways to eliminate this problem.

In 1974, a Love China Conference was held in Manila. Hundreds of missionaries and nationals concerned about China were there discussing ways to reach the 800 million people behind the Bamboo Curtain. Criticism of mission efforts in the past was brought forth and frankly considered. If China opens again to the missionary, what shall he do and how shall he approach this opportunity? Much of the criticism is centered around the life-style of the missionaries, and the lack of identification with the national.

Admittedly, some of the criticism is born of jealousy for the Western technology and consumer goods. However, our point is not to explain or defend but to figure out some way to identify with them. This the national can do, and his potential of winning his own people is tremendous, if we are willing to "loose him and let him go."

It's not only the life-style, but the whole thinking

pattern toward economics in general that provides distinctive ministries. Why is Asia so poor and Europe and America so wealthy? The reasons would fill a good sized book, and much of the material would have to do with attitudes toward wealth. The Westerner looks upon wealth as a tool to produce more wealth. The Asian looks upon the goods at his disposal merely as a commodity to be consumed and enjoyed. Religion, ideology, family and clan pressure, economic castes and government, plus many other factors are dedicated in certain areas to keeping the people impoverished. Exploding population growth renders almost useless the advances that are made. According to the *Reader's Digest* (February 1977), Mexico is growing at a rate four times faster than the United States. A new school classroom is added every thirty minutes. However, during the same period of time, 160 babies are born. All of these things combine to keep the rich growing richer, and the poor are left to suffer.

Nationalism is thought to be the most powerful factor in Asia today. This is a consciousness of belonging to a special group. Nationalism opposes outside interference, directing it's anger toward the Western world. Westerners consume most of the oil; they exploit cheap labor; they control the markets; and the flow of money is always through the Westerner's hands. The national sees himself as being poor because of them and they are purposefully keeping it this way. He believes that his rising standard of living will force the wealthier Westerner to give way. Right or wrong, these are his feelings. This can be supported or opposed by the religions of the country. Religion and ideology are important elements in the success or failure of Asia and Africa. These elements must be controlled, or at least pacified, if inroads are to be made. The Western missionary may have severe limitations placed on his ministry because of these factors. The unnoticed national, however, can still do much to promote Christianity in these circumstances.

The national can also relate Christianity to the culture in a nonthreatening way. Other people love their customs, habits, and traditions, just as the American loves Thanksgiving, football, and visiting old friends. They have their pattern of singing, worshiping, and meeting together. "Amazing Grace" may fit in or it may be sung to a new tune. Our order of service may not fit the nipa-housed community. Be assured the missionary will introduce it, and thus Christianity becomes "foreign," whereas the national is better equipped to adapt it to their society.

The story of Kho-Thah-Byu and Adoniram Judson is a lovely picture of a dedicated missionary and a working national. Judson had labored many years with little concrete results. He heard of the Karen tribe, far in the interior of Burma. In 1828 he found Kho-Thah-Byu, a Karen tribal man who had lived a vicious and brutal life as a slave for fifty years. It was reported that he had killed thirty people with his own hands. Judson paid the ransom and took him as a servant. Daily he taught and instructed the man until his darkened mind was enlightened by the story of the cross. He was baptized and went immediately to tell the same story to his people. For the next twelve years he traveled among the half-million Karens. Whole villages were converted, and it was said that forty thousand Karens were believers because of the ministry of this man.

The missionary is important, but a ministry of teaching and preaching must be committed to the converts of missionaries just as soon as it is possible. To hold tight to the gospel message, to refuse to let the national share in the ministry, is to invite an anemic, ill-equipped believer into a field ripe for the harvest. Many a Kho-Thah-Byu has been kept on the bench, refused permission to enter the missionary's game, and the resulting score has been dismal and often disastrous.

The stratification of converts is less likely to occur when the national is in the forefront of evangelism. Paternalism will not become a factor, and differences between the evangelist and the evangelized will not be as striking. Christianity is presented best when it is presented without the cultural trappings of a certain nation. It is sad to see the popularity of Christianity wax and wane with the popularity of America in some particular nation. China used this argument very effectively in 1949, and the Western missionaries were forced to leave as Christianity came under fire, just as the capitalist nations did.

Inevitably, as Christianity is presented, certain reforms must take place in a given society. Child brides, foot binding, polygamy, and other social ills must give way. There is a certain disturbance caused by the salty tang of the gospel. The missionary, even with the best intentions, has been the harbinger of a certain amount of social and moral chaos. Aggressive campaigns have been waged to get the primitive man to conform quickly to our mores and often to our economic pattern. Jesus told the story of a house swept clean of demons and then left empty. Soon the vacuum was filled by demons of a worse sort, and the last state of the house was worse than the first. As the old social ills are swept away, we must be cautious lest a worse malady fills the vacuum.

The national Christian, leading this kind of people, will be as successful and far less likely to introduce the foreign elements. The central ministry of the missionary, or foreign worker, may serve as the catalyst to assist in drawing the believers together, training them for service, and then encouraging their unique ministry.

In America, we are "community oriented," whereas the Orientals are family or "clan oriented." I have seen communities where the men could have dug a well in a weeks time. Instead, they let the women walk to the nearest stream and carry the water. The digging of a well would not have been a clan venture, therefore it was not considered. You see, there are few improvements in the Oriental village unless it is a government sponsored project. Community progress such as clean streets, parks, and other conveniences used by the public, is not really the concern of the clan.

The clan or family unit is that unique "family tree," and every person must belong to one. It becomes his security, his insurance policy, the old-age survivors benefit program, the burial policy, and his general welfare. He is bound by its laws and customs. He is obedient to the elders of the clan and will respect their decisions. His salary can be tapped for use by the clan, and when he is jobless the clan will feed him. A man's allegiance, then, is naturally toward the clan, not the community.

In many Asian villages, the clan arranges marriages for the young people. They are willing to accept this decision about their life's partner. The wisdom of the elders is considered much greater than the wisdom of two young people who are "in love." It is best to be matched properly and then the falling in love can take place. A young girl or a widow will have a difficult time finding a mate without the sanction of the clan. It is essential that she be a part of a clan to achieve social acceptance in her world.

When the elders of the clan are believers, you will find many believers in the clan. If the elders are opposed to Christianity, there will be few, if any, believers in the family. The clan must be considered in making any decision. Marriage, occupation, job-changing, moving to a new locale, and many other decisions are based on the ruling of the clan.

The national evangelist, or pastor, is aware of this. In fact, he is a believer in it and a part of it. He can move a clan toward becoming Christian, whereas the missionary may be working with an individual. If the individual becomes a believer, he could be "excommunicated" from the clan, making it difficult for him to survive. The national can present the message in a way that will harmonize with local customs, possibly with much less irritation and a more genuine response.

The lament of many clan elders today is the breakdown of this system. It has been shattered in many urban areas and the old Japanese, Chinese, or Korean elder can be seen shaking his head in utter amazement at the conduct of their people. Western ways, Western movies, and television, and a wider exposure to the world has caused a small revolution in this area. The clan is breaking down in the city, and the world is moving much too fast for them. In this transition, the stabilizing influence of the gospel could be of much help. Missionaries have been known to attack this system, and were in open defiance of the rulings of the elders. It is in this context where the national Christian worker may be able to achieve his finest ministry. He has the distinct advantage over the missionary in language, identification, and understanding. We need to encourage him to use it well in his environment.

Again it would bear repeating. The use of national workers does not make the missionary obsolete. He is needed and will continue to be needed in pioneer work, in teaching and training, in church development, and many other ministries where his talents can be used. Hopefully, we are aware that the national has an advantage over the missionary in certain areas, and that we will encourage him to exercise his abilities to the fullest.

Reflection #8

Bombay, India, is not considered the loveliest place, even in the bright sunlight. At 2:30 in the morning the qualities of beauty were scarcely improved. I sat in the big 747 with 392 others awaiting takeoff. My shoes were off, a blanket was spread over me, and I was looking forward to sleeping until we landed at Tel Aviv, Israel.

About halfway down the runway the pilot aborted the takeoff and brought the plane to a shuddering stop. From a reflection on the engine I could see that the wheels were on fire, and soon the smoke and flames were coming into the cabin. People began to scream and some raced up the aisles. The crew then popped open the ten emergency doors and all of us scrambled to safety. I left my briefcase, my camera, and of course, all my luggage in the plane. When I looked back, there were flames behind each of the small windows the entire length of the airplane. Seconds later the fuel tanks exploded.

People were numb with shock. A few seconds later and we would have been airborne where escape would have been most difficult. They took us to various hotels where we spent the remainder of the night. I recall the next morning as one of the low points of my life. I was twelve thousand miles from home, no clothes except what I wore, no comb, no toothbrush—nothing except a photostatic copy of a letter saying I had been on the ill-fated plane. I wanted to read from the Bible but mine had burned and the Gideons had not reached that hotel. Finally, I just quoted from the twenty-third Psalm and the words, "thy rod and thy staff they comfort me" (v. 4). In the depth of despair I knew I needed this comfort.

However, instead of comfort I was discomforted as the Lord seemed to rebuke me rather sharply. Here I was a Christian, supposedly a missionary, and if I felt this way how must the other passengers feel. Most of them were not Christians and probably had never heard the true gospel of Jesus. Immediately, I turned to a man in the room and apologized to him for being so distant. I told him my name and my business, and shared with him the good news of Christ. Soon I was speaking with another, a twenty-year-old lad from Vietnam, who said he heard that Christ died for him the first time that morning. We had to spend several days in India, and I spent what time I could trying to say something, or do something, or be something, that would help someone.

It dawned upon me as we flew out of India that I never did receive that promised comfort until I began to comfort others. Somehow, that which I sought to pass on into the lives of others was that which came back into my own life. I now had a small bag with a razor, a comb, and a small towel. But it's not the size of the suitcase that determines the comfort and the joy of the Lord, it's the size of the service rendered in his name.

8.
Mission Methods
You Need to Know

The Bible is not a manual on mission methods. It does command us to go, to make disciples, to baptize them, and to teach them. There is mass evangelism in the New Testament, but the one-on-one method can also be found. They went from house to house daily preaching the Word. They preached in established institutions, in the synagogues, and by the riverside. Philip went to the desert to witness to one man, and Paul was hopeful of being a city evangelist in Rome. Ethnic evangelism was spotlighted as Paul declared he would go to the Gentiles and Peter to the Jews. Jesus sent the twelve through the countryside and had them report back. John the Baptist was a brush-arbor man and Jesus enjoyed social occasions, even with the wine-bibbers. Street preaching, house preaching, using the boat as his pulpit with an outdoor cathedral, preaching from Pilate's judgment hall, and while hanging on the cross, Jesus was ever preaching. The methods varied according to the circumstances.

Paul declared he was willing to become all things to all men in order to bring the gospel to them. I suspect he was willing to use almost any method that was honorable. He was not strictly a foreign missionary nor did he limit his ministry, even though he claimed to be the apostle to the Gentiles. Basically, he went to the large cities and began to work with the Jews. When they were antagonistic, he turned to the Gentiles. It appears that strategy was not an inflexible plan with Paul. He left his plans open to the Holy Spirit and circumstances.

Let's take notice of Paul's missionary career. Please keep in mind there were few established churches, no sending boards for foreign missionaries, and the mission concept itself was strange.

1. Paul received a definite call for this work (Acts 13:1–2).

2. He conferred not with flesh and blood. That is, he did not discuss it with the church leaders in Jerusalem (Gal. 1:16).

3. He chose his fellow workers and argued heatedly about who would go with him (Acts 15:37).

4. He took offerings from one church to help another (Acts 11:27).

5. He worked as a tentmaker to support himself, though he plainly stated that they which preach the gospel should live by the gospel (1 Cor. 9:14).

6. He made periodic missionary journeys (Acts 15:36).

7. He claimed that God commanded him to go to the Gentiles (Acts 13:46).

8. He established churches and appointed elders or pastors (Acts 14:23).

9. He reported back to the church that sent him out (Acts 14:27).

10. He attended conferences and conventions and strongly defended his work (Acts 15).

11. He respected the religions of other people (Acts 17:22 ff).

12. He organized a church and stayed with it for a year and six months (Acts 18:11); for three years (Acts 20:31).

13. He returned to strengthen the churches he had started (Acts 18:23).

14. Paul never hesitated to claim his Roman citizenship when needed (Acts 22:28).

15. Paul had money to rent his own house (Acts 28:30).

The missionary methods of Simon Peter or James could also be listed. While it would be interesting, it would not set forth a "one method only" philosophy. Around the turn of the century, Roland Allen threw mission methodology into an uproar. He made a study of Paul's methods and then compared them with the methods being used in his day. Most methods, then as now, had been formulated by circumstances or expediency. Missions vacillated between one extreme or another. Allen, along with others, summed up Paul's methods as going where the Spirit led without any preconceived plan. He looked for the open door, chose a central place for the gathering of converts and the propagating of the faith, and had a definite aim of converting people to the new faith. Then he planted self-supporting churches and moved on to another location. The churches were left to grow by the power of God. They were not to be dominated by foreign personnel or supported by foreign funds.

Since then there have been many variations of these methods. Moreover, the methods have changed from country to country with modernization and levels of education. John Nevius, of China, came to Korea in 1890 and introduced a method that had not worked well in China, but was very fruitful in Korea. The Nevius Plan was to employ no paid workers, to teach the converts to tithe, and to stress a consistent Bible study.

John Geddi has to be given the prize for effective methods. There is a monument in the New Hebrides Islands in the South Pacific that claims there were no Christians on the island when he came and no heathen there when he left.

For many years the mission station approach was used. A compound was built, consisting of missionary houses, a church, a school, or some other institution. Converts were usually made one by one and brought inside to live, or given a job in the compound. Christianity became all foreign to the new believers, and they were removed from their natural setting. These "hot house plants" would thrive for a season, but when transplanted back into the native soil they would die or show little growth.

The teaching of Donald A. McGavran has affected mission methods greatly in the last decade. He observes that Paul did not choose fields so much but turned to responsive groups. These responsive groups were bridges and the gospel traveled on these bridges to reach others. He calls it a people movement. His keen observation is valid, and has inspired many missions to seek out the responsive people.[1]

The methods used are many. What produces much

fruit in one land may be barren in another. Modern technology has demanded a hearing. Radio, television, the airplane, even the computer are now being used. This will bring on additional methods. The strategy is to make the gospel known to every man, and it will not change. In reality it's not the method but the message that counts. The starving man in the desert sun is concerned about water. He is not apt to argue about the container, nor how it was brought to him. However, if there were ten thousand men dying rapidly of thirst and plenty of water was available, then the water and the method of serving would take on added importance.

When, where, and how should foreign funds be used? Arguments have waged for years over this. There are missionaries who believe that the more funds you have, the more work you can do. You can buy land, build a building, hire a pastor, and be in business in a few weeks. Frequently, they can point to a thriving church started in this way. The other extreme is to adopt the principle that no foreign funds will be used for any of these things. In between are those who believe that funds can be like a "charcoal starter," use a little to get the fire going and then discontinue it.

I heard a Chinese pastor in Hong Kong say that foreign subsidy is like taking a baby around on your back. The child needs help at first but after awhile he needs to walk. To carry the child on your back for five, ten, or fifteen years means he may never walk. Foreign funds can place a church on crutches and it will never walk.

Perhaps a larger danger is what it says to the national.

Subsidy says this is the way you begin a church. "You first take some money. . . ." Thus, in effect, we are saying the national, who seldom had money in the past, cannot begin new churches. Only the missionary can do that. Initative, mission outreach, and new innovativeness of the national is thwarted. Quickly, they become like the person who said, "I can't witness to him, I don't have a 'Four Spiritual Laws' booklet with me." We limit the growth, the evangelistic fervor, and the extension of Christianity by an unwise use of subsidy.

The best way of using funds is not easy to find. There are missions and national conventions who supposedly save years by moving in, and with the help of foreign funds, build churches, schools, organize a convention, and have the work moving forward. To have done this without the use of funds would have taken decades. "We have it, they need it, so why not use it?"

If subsidy is used, it would be well to have a program of national participation so they can share in it. If you have a foreign missionary using foreign funds to build a foreign building, you can bet it will remain foreign to the national. I well recall a letter I received from a pastor on one occasion. His church had been built with foreign funds. He wrote, "Your building is leaking badly and is in need of repair. When will you come to repair it?"

Subsidy, if used, should be a "one time" thing and not a continuing year-by-year grant. One church in South America claims the world record by receiving pastoral support for twenty-eight years. Some missions require the church to give "matching funds" in accordance with the amount granted by the mission. Somehow this is to be the best of both worlds and enables a church to grow rapidly. Loan boards, funded by foreign money, are used in some missions. This means a church meeting the requirements can usually borrow building money at little or no interest.

Money can create as many problems as it solves when used for direct subsidy. Moreover, it gives to the national the idea that money will solve all his problems. I was told once by a national that he wanted his country to become a Christian nation. He observed that America was a Christian nation and God had made them rich. "If my country is Christian, God will bless us like he did America."

The presence of a layman or evangelist from the States presents a tempting target for the national. Here is a businessman or at least a man with means. He is rich, or else he could not have made such a trip. "I will ask him to help me for my need is very great." Meanwhile, the layman is undergoing some degree of cultural shock, not to mention jet lag. He has been amazed at the number of people, strange customs, habits, language, and driving on the wrong side of the road. All of this has left him reeling. He has been shocked by the widespread poverty, slum areas, and beggars. He has some means and so reasons, "I'll do what I can."

This is a commendable spirit, and we are happy to see people give. It is still more blessed to give than to receive. It is good, along with our giving, to have some principles of giving. The old saying, "Give a man a fish and you feed him for a day, teach him to fish and you've fed him for a lifetime," is still true. The layman, like the career missionary, sees the need and in some manner tries to respond. I fervently hope this spirit never leaves us. Some people believe it is better to be deceived several times by fake beggars if you can help one beggar that is really in need.

One principle would be in inquiring how to give, how much to give, and to whom it should be given. How well I recall the problem of tithing in my early missionary days. The first church where I worshiped met in a small mud hut with rice straw mats for the floor. Their weekly offering amounted to thirty-five cents. My tithe for one month would have been more than the annual budget. In many mission field churches today, if one gives five dollars it will double the offering for that day. It's true that rice or other produce is often given in lieu of cash. If some stranger dumps twenty dollars in the offering plate it does upset the budget. One missionary doctor moving to a new city was besieged by the churches. They met him at the train, they all invited him to eat and to attend their church. Finally, one pastor, who felt like he was losing ground said, "But Sir, even if you can't come, just send your offering to our church." Stewardship principles and promotion must be kept in mind as we give.

A visiting stateside pastor was in a church overseas. All week long he watched the young pastor walk the dusty streets to visit. Perhaps there was something he could do. He decided to purchase a motorcycle for the pastor. The price of the motorcycle was the equivalent of two years salary for the lucky pastor. He was thrilled with it and wrote the layman a thank-you letter and soon was receiving regular contributions from the generous friend.

Meanwhile, eleven other pastors in the association, who also walked the dusty villages, wanted motorcycle funds. They besieged the area missionary for help, pointing out that he had no love for them unless some motorcycles were forthcoming. The missionary had no funds nor would the mission allow it even if funds had been available. Then they requested a crusade in their churches with foreigners to come and lead it. Also, none of the young pastor's flock had a motorcycle or a foreign source of funds. Jealousy and envy crept into the picture. The pastor devised a way of making a taxi tricycle out of the gift and made even more money. Soon his relatives, noting that he was now a wealthy businessman in the village, moved in on him seeking help for varied illnesses, fees for children's schooling, and relief in general. The last I heard he was in debt, his motorcycle was sold, and his influence had rapidly diminished in the community.

Stories could well be told of gifts given that resulted in really helping some poor pastor, and became a real blessing to the community. Giving of gifts is not condemned, but certain principles and mission policy should be considered. Will this really help the person? Will it advance the growth of the church? What is the custom about gifts in this country? What does the missionary advise about it? This is no plea for a tightfisted policy toward others, but more must be considered than the obvious need. Many good crusades have been hurt because of indiscriminate giving to nationals. This usually comes to light several weeks after the visitors have returned to the States. The missionary suddenly finds he has problems and wishes he had emphasized this more in the orientation meeting. Small gifts, in keeping with the economy, should be given to your host pastor and will be appreciated. However, the "my church will send you fifty dollars each month to help on your salary" attitude, can be contrary to established policies of the mission and provoke many problems.

Another sensitive zone is the invitation to national workers to come to the United States. The visitors may reason that he could get a better education there, solve his financial woes, and return to serve his people. It has happened this way, but the odds are against it. Some have been educated so well that they are unable to function in their society upon returning. They get accustomed to "things" that are out of place in their culture. Frequently they become bitter and disappointed because of the shortcomings of their country as they compare it with America. They try to lord it over their fellow nationals because they have been educated in the United States.

It can be pointed out that there are nationals, educated in the U.S., who are now the leaders in their countries. They are fine pastors and most useful to the Kingdom's work because of their training. However, chances are that for everyone who returns and proves to be useful in his native land, there will be four, or eight, or even ten, who do not return to assist in the evangelizing of their nation. This is by no means a plot to keep the national from going to the U.S. Some should go, but they should be carefully selected by the mission or the national convention. As a rule, they are in much better position to ascertain the talents and future usefulness of the individual.

The visitor in many countries will be besieged by people wanting to get to the United States. Long lines can be seen in front of the American embassy. They may need only a "sponsor." The visitor is impressed by their zeal, their strong motivation to serve the Lord. "My church would be happy to help a fellow like that," they reason. Percentagewise the results are not too favorable. The nationals lose a worker, other nationals are not pleased if one is favored above the others, and the chances of him ever returning are not too great.

Southern Baptists have spent thousands of dollars for seminaries. Some of our most talented missionaries are teaching in them. Instruction is geared to the country where he lives and where he will serve. They can usually attend a Christian college and seminary nearby and receive a good education. If graduate work is advisable, there are regional graduate schools or the mission and convention may decide to send him to the U.S. for further study. The national worker, with only a Bible school certificate, is more valuable to the mission program in his country than the national who has earned a doctorate in the U.S. and is still residing in Honolulu or California. I realize that many people will take exception to this and be able to quote beautiful illustrations of how successful their venture was in this area. Exceptions to most rules of this nature can be cited, but usually the best procedure is for the national to take advantage of the educational facilities in his own country.

Mission work in some countries has been done through institutions such as hospitals, schools, or special projects. Indeed, in certain areas this is the only way the missionary can gain entrance. The method can be the most expensive, but it is also the most humanitarian. It is desperately needed in neglected sections of the world. You can find the lowly fifty-bed mission hospital serving a half million people, missionary doctors and nurses working eighteen hours a day reaching people who would never be reached through a regular church program. Much the same could be said for schools, social centers, and agricultural ministries. However well they may function, from time to time, the total thrust of the mission program must be examined. Just because a hospital was needed in 1925 doesn't mean it can be justified today. Can the national ever hope to operate the institution? Is the purpose humanitarian only? Are churches being planted? What part will such an institution be having in the total mission thrust in the future?

Evangelism is best when the evangelized become evangelists. The most thrilling thing on the mission horizon is the national churches which are beginning to send out missionaries. For years mission work has been the "white man's burden." There are hopeful signs that national churches are realizing their own responsibility in this area. This has been long in coming, and much of the fault must lie at the feet of the mission- ary. This has usually been the last doctrine presented to a mission field church. Stewardship, soul-winning, the Sunday School, plus the doctrine of sin, salvation, and the second coming, are given as regular teachings of the church. One national was visiting in the U.S. and heard a missionary speak who had been serving in his home country. He had heard him preach many times, but always in the distant land. He was amazed to hear the missionary preach about missions and the response. The missionary presented the need and chal- lenged the entire congregation. No sooner had the mis- sionary finished than the national rushed forward and ask, "Why have you never preached this to my people?"

The Great Commission belongs to the forty-member mission field church just as much as it does to the old First Baptist Church, U.S.A. Why should they be robbed of the precious task of laboring where the fields are white unto harvest? Worldwide evangelism is a church task, not just an American or European task. Can the Holy Spirit use a brown or a black missionary? There is something basically wrong with a church which has no missionary outreach.

Thankfully, the picture is changing and overseas churches are beginning to send missionaries. In 1973, there was an All-Asia Consultation of Missions held in Seoul, Korea. Problems, personnel, and opportunities were discussed. Prior to 1960 very few Third World people had gone forth as missionaries. Now the Church Growth Study Center reports 196 sending agencies in forty-four countries sending out 2,971 missionaries.[2] Admittedly, some of these are ethnic missionaries coming to the U.S.A. to minister to their own people. The word "foreign" has little meaning to these people as they seek to major on missions, not on the foreign aspect. Also, much of the fund-raising is carried on in American churches.

The thrilling part, however, is that there is an awakening among the mission field churches to reach out to others. They want to share in world evangelism and they make excellent missionaries. The ability to get the language quickly and adapt to the ways of a new country has been noted by all concerned. I heard a Korean telling how quickly he was able to mix with the Vietnamese. The similarities in life-style, the quick grasp of their language, and the zeal of the Third World missionary to prove he could do it made a great impact on the missionaries and nationals.

Many missions are beginning to reevaluate their approach to sending boards on what we have labeled as the "mission fields." There are still hundreds of islands in the South Pacific without a Baptist witness. Tribes in the high rain forest without Scripture portions, villages without churches, and rampant evil and superstition can still be found in heartbreaking numbers. To reach these people will take the entire resources of the Christian Church. Our brown and black brothers can make a mighty contribution, and we could live to see the day when they will be more welcomed by the world community than the traditional white missionary.

Strategy and methods are important on the mission field. However, they are not the most important thing. A genuine willingness to be used by the Lord will enable any missionary to learn the best methods. The dedicated player on the football field can be taught the strategy of the game and the execution of the plays. It's the willingness that counts. We do well, in the final analysis, to recall the strategy laid down by our Lord: "Go ye therefore, and teach all nations, baptizing them in the name of the Father, and of the Son, and of the Holy Ghost: Teaching them to observe all things whatsoever I have commanded you: and, lo, I am with you alway, even unto the end of the world. Amen" (Matt. 28:19–20).

[1] Donald A. McGavran, *The Bridges of God* (London: World Dominion Press, 1957), p. 4.

[2] Clyde W. Taylor, "Overseas Churches Starting to Send Missionaries," *Evangelism Mission Quarterly,* Vol. 10, No. 1 (January 1974), p. 61.

Reflection # 9

Both of them had a tired look when they entered our home. They were young missionaries who, before coming to the field, had to raise their salaries in pledges from various churches. They often refer to themselves as "faith missionaries." We had invited them to our home for a quiet dinner party and they really seemed grateful. Immediately the wife said, "I am just tired out. I've been writing letters all day to our supporting people and churches. Several have dropped out and our income is so low that we hardly know what to do. My arm is about to drop off."

Later in the evening the husband shared with us some of his anxiety and fear. He was unable to pursue his plans for a Bible school. He was worried about paying the school fees for his two children. He was in the throes of a financial nightmare that was draining the joy of service out of his life.

After they left, we began to think about our support, our school fees, and the future of our work. I remembered the Cooperative Program and the thousands of Baptists who participated in our ministry by giving each Sunday to their local church budget. Faithful deacons and finance committees had been guided to give more and more each year to our mission program.

I had a lot to thank the Lord for that night. I didn't lie awake wondering who I could ask to help support me. My school fees had already been paid. The fear and anxiety of the perplexed young missionary was unknown to Southern Baptists. We too are faith missionaries. We have faith that God will use Southern Baptists to continue to pray, to give, and to go.

Thank you, Lord, that my wife does not have to spend several days each month writing letters, begging people to support us in our mission work.

9.
The Layman and Mission Support

There was a time when the steward "ship" had rough sailing across the sea of American religion. Pastors were underpaid, churches were in debt, and mission programs were anemic. A speaker would come to the associational meetings of churches and make high-pressured appeals for his school, orphanage, or his special project. He would be followed by another, then another. Soon there followed a great stress on tithing. In 1925 the Cooperative Program was created as a way to meet the needs of our institutions and mission programs in which each church could have a part. As America prospered, Baptists gave more, churches multiplied, and most Baptist institutions grew. For many, stewardship was interpreted as giving, of which the tithe was the ultimate.

Through all of this, there were men who championed the cause of biblical stewardship as being more, much more. However, it has been in this decade that we have recognized, and hopefully accepted, stewardship as a way of life. It is a way of life, or a life-style tailored to our Christian commitment. Stewardship is not merely tithing on Sunday, it is managing one's assets seven days a week so as to honor the Creator. It means that every circumstance in our life gives evidence that we belong to our Master and we act as his servant. It means that all relationships are entered into with a full knowledge of our accountability to God. The tithe is holy, but so is the 90 percent. The 10 percent tip to the church is without true spiritual meaning unless the 90 percent is used aright. Thus, man becomes a spiritual overseer of all the possessions entrusted to him. It is as a slave or a servant who awaits the coming of his master, and then he will give an accounting for all his stewardship. If he has spent ten hours on the golf course, two hours in church, and no hours serving his fellowman, then he will be called to account for it. If he has given a tithe to his church, then used the surplus for a boat, a summer cottage, or a television for every room, then he must account for it. This is no condemnation of material possessions. Some fisherman had a boat that Jesus used, and some man let him use the upper room of his house, and a lad gave him his lunch. He never condemned the holding of possessions but he did speak pointedly about man's attitude toward these possessions. There is a distinctive Christian view of material goods that honors Christ in the totality of all that we possess. It comes into focus when we trade for a new car, buy a second stereo, or purchase the weekly groceries. It is saying, "Lord, as your servant, I want to use my possessions entrusted to my care, to honor your name and to extend your Kingdom."

As Baptists, we have long been bumping our heads

on the tithe as the ceiling in Christian giving. Recently, a church in a Western state had a new emphasis placed on stewardship. They really came to see themselves as involved in a global witness—a partnership with the Lord. Offerings zoomed as members pondered how little they could get by on and how much they could give. Some were soon giving 40 percent, some 50 percent, and some over 60 percent of their income.

In a true sense they had broken a "sound barrier." They had shaken free of the gravitational pull of the tithe. We have made the tithe the ceiling rather than the foundation of our giving. We are law-bound rather than love-bound. Thus, mentally we are constantly butting our heads on that 10 percent ceiling. Religiously we give our tithe, pay our bills, put a small amount in savings, and then discover we have a surplus. Now, since we have met our religious obligation, we surmise that we can do as we please with the remainder. We often trip over this 10 percent syndrome on the way to the boat sale, the beach cabin, or to various amusements. However, we are only shaken for a moment as we claim the 10 percent blessing and rush on with our surplus. We have kept the law, we are paid up on our church pledge, what more can be expected of us? We even grow to like this. It is quite easy to tip the tithe and be relieved of that awesome responsibility of being a faithful steward. Was this not the very attitude Jesus condemned in Matthew 23?

God has richly blessed Southern Baptists. This means our responsibility has multiplied. With the tithe as our springboard, and not as the ceiling, we could truly make "as the Lord has prospered you," rather than "the tithe," our guide in giving. In other words, our standard of living should be determined by God's will and not by our income. This places stewardship on a solid biblical basis and not just on tithing. It places man as a trustee over all possessions in his care, including a will for the distribution of his estate after death.

Is not a child of the King a member of the Kingdom? Motivated by love, the Kingdom's interest should be his major concern. As long as we see the tithe as the ultimate in Christian giving, we will keep bumping our heads on the ceiling. The knots on our head will hardly be worthy trophies to set before our Lord.

The stewardship way is not a choice of giving or not giving, tithing or not tithing, but a recognition of our management duty in the matter of posssessions entrusted to us. It's not a question of seeing the needs of our church or the needs of the world, but of seeing our position as a steward in the Master's house.

As an individual, what can the layman do in mission support? What is it that we expect our money to accomplish on the mission field? We want the sick healed, the weary comforted, the hungry fed. We want the gospel proclaimed to every man, with churches being established that will continue this ministry. These are the very things we should be involved in where we live. Have we the right to expect our money to do something overseas that we will not do in our hometown? The happiest Christian is the serving Christian. Most conditions of the foreign fields can be found near where you live. It may vary in degrees, but there is poverty, superstition, and unbelief all around us. When you lift up your eyes, there is the mission field.

Prayer support is vital. Think not that the Kingdom will be ushered in by the finance department. We are engaged in spiritual warfare that causes us to realize our strength is from the Lord. Once I asked a deep sea diver what the most important thing in the world was when you are a hundred feet or more under the water. Without hesitation he told me it was the oxygen line from the ship to his diver's helmet. He declared that the main thing was to keep it clear, unbent, and flowing. "Nothing I find, nothing I do, nothing I discover, is as important as protecting that lifeline," was his statement.

The lifeline for the believer is prayer and the devotional life. Nothing we do is as important as keeping that line open. Jesus said, "I am the vine, ye are the branches; He that abideth in me and I in him, the same bringeth forth much fruit, for without me ye can do nothing" (John 15:5). The real secret of fruit bearing is abiding. The same secret applies to Christian workers in the homeland or overseas. Pray that out missionaries will continue to abide in Christ. Pray for our national leaders as they seek to serve in their homeland. Pray for the work and workers listed in the various mission magazines. How much it means to a missionary to get a letter from an individual or Sunday School class that is praying and encouraging him in his work.

In the old farmer's cabin the frost would gather on the window so the children could not see out. They would scrape if off but soon it would again cover the window. Finally the farmer said, "Let yon window alone me lads, and kindle the fire. That will take care of the frost." We catch ourselves trying to make ready the work of our Lord. We apply organization, resources, and modern ingenuity, but what we really need is to kindle the flame of prayer. So many of the problems melt away in such heat.

One thing that is dearly appreciated in Southern Baptists is the support of all our work. We need to support our state mission programs, the youth assemblies, the Christian colleges, and seminaries. To neglect this is to neglect our mission program. I am convinced that we maintain a strong overseas emphasis because there is a strong support of our state and national causes. It may be the mission group leader who will first open the eyes of a young child to the world. He is sent to a camp supported by your state and the view is confirmed. Trained in a Baptist college and seminary, he is now ready to go and exercise his gifts. Weaken all these programs and you will weaken our world ministry. "I don't give to these state programs, I support our missionaries," are not the wisest words. Designated giving to only one segment of the mission program may be a step backwards into the days of the high-pressured speaker, seeking funds for his particular program.

In the budget committee or finance meeting, what is the real value of a layman saying, "Fellows, let's raise our percentage of giving this year to our total mission program"? His words indicate a concern for world missions. The people in the United States need the gospel just as those in Africa. What is the value of a layman making a tour of the mission fields in the Northwest, or to a foreign field? He sees the need, he is impressed with how much is being done, and world missions has a supporter in that local church. Owen Cooper, former president of the Southern Baptist Convention, has pointed out that laymen are appalled to learn how little their church is really giving to world causes. Once they connect this giving with the world ministry, there is a determination to do more. Some laymen use their vacations to visit mission work among the migrant workers. Professional men give a month or more to working in Mexico, Africa, or the slums of a city in America. It all amounts to world awareness at the family breakfast table, at the shop during the day, and in a budget committee meeting that night.

Strong home churches are necessary for strong mission work overseas. The grass-roof chapel in Africa is but an extension of the ministry of your church. The stronger your home church is in evangelism, stewardship, and outreach ministries, the stronger will be the churches overseas. The layman can see that missions is constantly kept before the church. Missionaries and denominational workers can be invited to speak and present the work being done. Efforts can be made to get the men as interested and informed on missions as the ladies' missionary societies. Prayer features can be used to relate the Sunday offerings to how it will be used locally and around the world. Mission magazines and denominational papers are most useful to every family in the church.

Churches, informed and aware of the world evangelism outreach, are led to give $75.00 or $100.00 per capita to outside causes. How does this compare with the $3.70 given by each Baptist in 1974? The real problem is not the per capita giving, but the fact that an estimated 50 percent of Southern Baptists gave little, if any, to mission causes. Our churches need to be made aware of this and laymen can do it. One layman said that he had never heard of a church giving 20 percent, or 25 percent to mission causes outside the church that had financial problems. It is when missions is neglected that churches have to turn to glorified begging, or cake walks and bingo parties. Rumors have it that one church in Africa voted to lower the tithe from 10 percent to 5 percent. Whether this solved their economic dilemma is not made clear.

William Carey, father of modern missions, was inspired by the Moravians. At one time this church had one missionary on the foreign field for every fifty-eight members in the home church. Just think what Southern Baptists could be doing with over thirteen million members.

The point is not to minimize what we are now doing. We thank God that Baptists continue to give and support mission work in eighty-three countries. Other mission boards and agencies are cutting back while we are launching a program to expand. However, it does no harm to realize that the total budget of the Foreign Mission Board would not buy four Tomcat fighter planes for the U.S. Navy. Total giving of all Southern Baptists to outside causes could not equal what we spend on one attack submarine. The average Baptist will spend more this year on chewing gum and soft drinks than he will give to foreign missions. Often he is just not aware of his stewardship and the claim of God upon his life and his life-style.

It is at this point where the layman can do so much in keeping his church abreast of the world mission causes. William Carey learned of the need, and his heart was stirred to do something. Luther Rice saw the need, and was stirred to give his life to mission support. What would be the effect of having our layman stirred by the need and the claims of our Lord for evangelizing all the world?

Reflection #10

I had driven the rough Land-Rover over the corrugated Korean roads for most of the day. My back ached, my eyes burned, and my mind was centered on some good American food, and a tall, cool glass of iced tea that awaited me at home. As we neared the city of Taegu the traffic became heavier. Taxis, busses, and hap-sungs (a semibus) were vying for choice customers as they darted in and out of the main traffic stream. Were I a profane man, I'm sure I would have addressed some choice remarks to the hap-sung driver in front of me as he would pull over a little, but never enough for me to pass. Each time one or two passengers would quickly get on or off. Finally we almost collided as he pulled over and I started around him. Both of us had to stop to prevent an accident. Leaning over I shouted a few well-chosen insults at him, using the low form of Korean speech. Instantly, he got out of the bus, bowed low and with very polished Korean, apologized for being in my way. The cigarettes in his shirt pocket indicated to me that he was not a believer. (I've never known of a Korean believer smoking.)

Now if there is anything that makes me mad, it is for an unbeliever to out-Christian me. This pagan had certainly shown more attributes of the Holy Spirit than I had. By this act of courtesy and kindness this hap-sung driver had heaped some red hot coals on my head. Arguing, fussing, name-calling, I could have understood. But this kind spirit that possessed the tired, hard-pressed hap-sung driver, put me to shame. I know the impression he made on me, and shamefully, I fear that I know the kind of impression I made on him.

10.
Things That Hurt

Americans have been seen and heard around the world more than any other nationality. For the most part we are still liked and the dollar, though losing ground, is still favored. Of course, there are those all to willing to remember the booming artillery shells falling on noncombatants, or the 220 pound American slapping the 100 pound bar-girl, or the drunk American commandeering the hotel elevators and refusing to let others use them. This also happens when nationals of any country live or visit another place. It was interesting to note the Egyptians list of grievances against the Russians a few years ago. Arrogance, seclusivism, and ignoring the Egyptian laws were at the top of the list.

Usually the missionaries and the nationals are thrilled to note the courtesy, kindness, and Christian spirit of the American visitors. They say the right things, compliment the host country, and go the second mile in public relations. This is as it should be, for the national is just as proud of his country as you are of your country. While the development of the miracle rice may not equal the scientific interest of walking on the surface of the moon, it is as important to the national as he points it out to his guest. The limping, slat-seated bus may not compare with the latest Greyhound but it will impress you . . . hopefully to remain silent.

Neither is it necessary to condemn all things American in trying to prove your love to the national. Americans have exported a lot of things that are wonderful. Electricity, the telephone, and the airplane were all invented or discovered by Americans and we don't have to apologize for it. Perhaps it is the odious comparisons that sting the hardest. I remember showing a visitor around one of the more interesting cities in the Orient. Every time I would point out an unusual sight he would counter with, "You know, we have one of those back in Hometown, USA, except ours is a lot larger." Mercifully, we cut the tour short that day.

In the Christian realm much more is expected of the visiting guest. The attitude of the visiting American is noted, his words are quoted, and his conduct reflects not only on America but also on Christianity. The East has long considered the Westerner as the barbarian. Even with all his vaunted technology, knowledge, and skill, he is still a ruffian in manners and the simple things that really matter. All the accomplishments of Western technology will pale as the Westerner picks up his food with his hand while a perfect set of chopsticks goes unused.

Even the worldly man expects more of the Christian. As the national told the businessman, "Yes, I can lie to him, but you can't for you are a Christian." The things that irritate you when foreigners visit the United States will probably irritate the national when you are in his country. Love and respect, two overworked words, are still a much-loved currency in the world market. The nationals everywhere recognize you are a foreigner, and that you have your own culture, mores, and education. He does expect or desire for you to become as he is. He does expect the differences between the nations to be respected. The foreigner berated the poor Oriental bussinessman for using a cheap bamboo abacus in adding up his bill. He demanded that he be permitted to add it up on his new pocket calculator. However, most all of us are surprised to learn of the longevity, the availability, and the accuracy of this ancient calculator. Usually there are good reasons why they do things in a certain way. It is best that we delay any advice or criticism until we have found out the situation.

The big red tractor works wonders on the huge farms in the Midwest. However, in Korea, where the farms are small, some less than two acres in size, it would not be too valuable. Also, the fields have to have dikes and irrigation ditches and only the ox can plow in the flooded fields. It is true the tractor could do the work of a hundred men. That may mean that a hundred men would join the unemployment ranks, for jobs are scarce. Had I known all of this I would not have asked the farmers why they didn't get a tractor. "Why don't they wear clothes, like they ought to?" or "How can they eat that stuff?" or "What a lazy bunch," may be answered best by some discreet observation. However, don't be shocked if they come to America and ask the same questions.

You can compile a list of things that will irritate the nationals and it would qualify for use in most every country in the world. Have you ever traveled around and heard some of the following echoes?

1. *Arrogance.*—You never say a word but your actions say, "I'm better than you are and nothing you have could possibly be as good as what I have."

2. *Exporting your culture.*—"My culture is so much superior. While you have some good qualities, naturally mine are better. I knew you wouldn't have any decent food so I brought my own."

3. *Paternalistic attitude.*—"Come, come my children, we are here to help you." "Isn't it amazing how all blacks can sing." "Our Japanese are such lovely people."

4. *Loud, brash, and a show-off.*—"Stand aside folks, the first team is here." "I left a Cadillac for that." "Here, take this and buy a round for everybody."

5. *Confusing patriotism with Christianity.*—This carries the idea that the two are the same. "We fought a war for your sake." "I don't care what they say, I'm going to have the American flag in our church."

6. *Impatience.*—"My time is so valuable. I can't waste time talking with those people. Come on, time is money. No tea sipping, no bowing, let's get out of here."

7. *Trying to do everything.*—This game is played by making the people dependent on you. Many nationals are born "leaners" (notice how I've fallen into the cliché bit) and once they find out they can lean on you there will be some confusion. They may be natu-

rally reticent and will always wait for you to lead. "I can do it quicker than I can tell someone else how" becomes our motto.

The list could go on. These are merely characteristics that the world does not like. Since Americans are usually the larger group of tourists, they are more frequently linked to them. It is well to note that we can hurt the feelings of the national and negate any good we might do by exhibiting these traits. Here again, the cure is love and respect, with a dash of information.

It is helpful to understand "culture shock" when we travel to a new country. This is the emotional disturbance caused by contact with a new environment. We have lost the familiar, and, like a child in a strange room, we withdraw and are uncertain. We are disoriented because our mind cannot compute all the strange sounds, foods, and mannerisms about us. We are fearful that we will miss a cue and throw everything into confusion. We long for the familiar. To recognize culture shock and understand its significance will enable you to make a speedy recovery.

The symptoms come in varied forms. It's what causes a man to walk by a dozen of the best restaurants in Paris to buy the familiar hamburger. It is the rejection of the host country and usually all that goes with it. If you get sick you must have an American doctor to treat you. Only American medicine is safe to take. You seek the isolation with the "all American" unit and shield yourself from the nationals. There may be the symptom of endless complaining about everything. Faultfinding is honed to its sharpest edge. Some will grow quiet and moody, another brash, and seek to compare everything to his hometown. The opposite may occur and you will hear a person rave about how much better everything is compared with what he had in the United States. Bitter feelings, imagined slights, and injustices can make mountains out of the social molehills. Feelings of guilt, hostility, inferiority, or superiority, may indicate the presence of culture shock.

Some of Coach Vince Lombardi's football players would say that the coach was impartial and "treats us all the same, just like dogs." This may help in developing a championship team but it will hurt your witness in a foreign country.

The biggest shock may be your own reaction to all of this. You begin to see a side of yourself that has never expressed itself before. There may be a case of weeping over a language problem; behaving like a spoiled child over the traffic situation; or shouting at a national because he cannot understand English. The halo begins to tarnish as you measure the depth of your Christian experience. Face it. Call it by name and resolve to do something about it. The emotional disturbance will fade like a summer cloud and you can enjoy the best of both continents.

Culture shock can be seen in reverse when a missionary returns for furlough and insists that everything in Masuganaland is better than in the United States. He is disoriented to his own hometown and all the gadgets, coin machines, credit cards, and the like leaves him longing for the familiar. The nationals of any country grow weary of hearing these superlatives after awhile.

Why all these comparisons anyhow? If one goes to Japan, he expects to see Japanese behaving in a Japanese way. You are part of your culture and it will take a long time to change that. You don't have to run down your country nor strain to prove it is perfect; just accept it.

The inability to recover from culture shock leads to more frustration and will hurt the witness of a believer. Try to conquer it. Read the available books on history, customs, and characteristics of the land where you will be visiting. A good sense of humor will go a long way. Learning to laugh at your own mistakes will keep you from dwelling too long on another's mistakes.

The smug assumption that the nationals can do nothing, but the American can do everything, is a bitter pill to swallow. This has spilled over into mission work and crusades. Nationals *can* sing, play musical instruments, and preach. They have ability to equal and often surpass the foreign in dealing with crowd psychology, teaching methods, and logistics. If they are constantly shut out, soon they will shut out the foreigner.

Perhaps there is another thing which can hurt the visitor in assisting the nationals in an evangelistic project or working in an institution. This could be called the "walking on eggshells" theory or always being fearful that you are going to offend the national. You ask about every little petty detail, you always wait for him to make the first move, you leave every decision up to him. After a while he feels that he is dealing with a machine or a terribly naive person. Common sense is best applied here and we are thankful that most overseas visitors are well-equipped in this area. In this area the Golden Rule, as taught by Lord, should ever be on our mind. With this as the motivation, even our mistakes can be turned into blessings.

Reflection #11

We had walked most of the morning, reaching the Maka-sila River on Mindanao Island just before noon. Across the river we could see the burned village of Bananal, an ugly assortment of scorched tin and blackened nipa. Rebel forces had come early one morning, firing their guns to warn the people to run, and then they burned the entire village of some two hundred people.

With a heavy heart we turned back toward the refugee settlement. They wanted me to meet the church treasurer. She was living in a lean-to with a dirt floor and came out to greet us warmly with a firm handshake. She told of the morning they came and how she had about thirty seconds to decide what to take. She wanted to take her clothes, then she thought of the family pictures, and then she remembered that she was the treasurer of the church. One man had recently given his tithe. It was a pig and was penned up near the house. She grabbed up the pig and ran from the flaming village.

Then she turned and pointed to the pig, now with seven little piglets and said, "I just wanted you to know, the Bananal Baptist Church is back in business."

11.
The Christian Woman on the Mission Field

The title of this chapter is not to indicate that women were excluded in the previous chapters. Usually, when the term *layman* was used, it was in a generic sense. Lay persons would have been more accurate, but we are more accustomed to the term *layman.* This chapter does indicate that there is a specific role on the mission field that can best be fulfilled by a woman. "I just came along with my husband" is modest enough but it is hardly an excuse for not entering into the various evangelistic opportunities that are presented.

In the Old Testament, the frequent mentioning of women is remarkable in light of their position in life at that time. Sarah, in effect, became the mother of the chosen nation. The lovely story of Rebekah and Rachel have valuable lessons for all of us today. And who will forget the contributions of Rahab and Ruth. Deborah and Huldah are called "prophetesses," and held positions commanding respect.

Perhaps one of the more interesting studies could be made in the New Testament concerning the women who followed Jesus. This thought came to me in a recent service where I noticed the ladies outnumbered the men considerably. Many reasons could be given for this. Some men were on the night shift, others were traveling, and some were unconverted. Then I recalled, that in the lean years of our local church, it was the ladies who practically pulled us through. Out on the Western frontier they seldom had churches, though saloons abounded, until the women arrived. It's not by chance that the two largest offerings of Southern Baptists are named after women. Youth camps, colleges, and special mission programs often owe their life, if not their birth, to some godly women.

It could be that the present time is not too different from biblical days. It was Rachel's daughters weeping when Herod killed the innocents. Jesus' mother "hid these things in her heart" and pondered them. Mary and Martha, the friendly possessors of a lovely home, often entertained Jesus and his disciples. Mary, and the other Mary, followed him to the cross, and it was a woman who heard the first announcement of the resurrection.

In the Epistles, names like Dorcas, Priscilla, and Phoebe were well known. The famed T.E.L. class is named after one man and two women (Timothy, Eunice, Lois). Paul, seemingly, had the utmost respect for services they performed in the church. His letters are filled with greetings to various women.

Church history is crowded with exploits of faithful women whose discipleship mirrors an era of bravery. At Calvary there were women in the background, revealing an inner strength that seemed to have failed some of the other followers of Jesus. The widow's mite is used to inspire others to give. Christ took note of it and commented on it. Apparently he had little or nothing to say about the giving of others that day. The widow's mite for Southern Baptists today has grown to be an offering that totaled more than twenty-five million dollars in 1976. Lottie Moon gave the mite, and millions have been inspired. This is no time to despise the day of small things.

In many countries women still have far less freedom than their Western counterparts. Their plight has long been noted by women of other nations. In 1888, some women in London created the first international organization for praying and taking an offering for missionary purposes. Their purpose was to help the twenty million widows in India. Faithful Christian women dedicated themselves to praying and giving with a universal scope in mind. They were carrying on the tradition of true service to their Lord, just as Dorcas and Priscilla had done two thousand years ago. They followed their husbands to the ends of the world, and often the home in the wilderness was carved by a woman's hand. They faced a hostile world, ruled by corrupt men who were dedicated to keeping women in an inferior position.

The liberating power of the gospel began to be felt. We often give mission field reports on the number of churches, pastors, and baptisms. Suppose you could see one that dealt with intangible results.

—One million tiny feet were not bound this year because missionaries have opposed it for one hundred and fifty years.

—500,000 widows did not throw themselves on the

funeral pyres of their husbands in India.

—There were few marriages of ten- and twelve-year-old children.

—Female babies were not left outside to freeze and older daughters were not sold into slavery and prostitution.

—No cheeks were slashed and filled with ashes to make scars.

—Headhunters were hunting game only.

—Nine- and ten-year-old children were not working twelve hours a day in sweatshops.

This is not to say that Christianity has been directly responsible for all of this. However, Christianity has denounced it for many years, and the influence of dedicated missionaries, male and female, had a measure of success in abolishing many of the social ills.

In matters of the heart it is more often the women who respond. They have given the widow's mite when the men could find nothing but criticism. Their arms have been opened to the orphans, the homeless, and the destitute in a fashion that has raised our thinking on the dignity of man. Phoebe is described in Romans 16:1 as a "servant of the church." From that day to our present time these "servants of the church" have added a quality of strength to the ministry of the church that has been felt worldwide.

Hanna Yang was seventy-five years old the last time I saw her. At one time she had been a wealthy woman, then came the Korean war in 1950, and she lost wealth and family. In the port city of Pusan she became concerned with the mentally ill people. Many of these were turned out to roam the streets, others were kept locked in dark rooms. Hanna said that she found one chained in a stable. She began to collect these people unto herself and offer them a home. Missionaries, the United States Army, and the Korean government helped when they could.

On Christmas day 1968, Hanna invited me to come and speak to the people in her home. It was a cold day, but the service was held outside in a courtyard. I noticed as I was speaking, that one lady moved slowly through the crowd to come and stand by Hanna Yang. She was a pitiful looking person. An old gray coat, about three sizes too large, was wrapped around her and tied with a cord. On the lapel was a cross. She had cut it out of cardboard and then used tinfoil from chewing gum wrappers to cover it. It was pinned to her lapel with a straight pin. Flashing in the wintry sun it was undoubtedly the ugliest, crudest thing you could imagine.

Then I asked of myself why she did it. Why a cross anyhow? What did this poor mentally afflicted person know about the cross or about the Christ who died on it? By this time Hanna Yang had reached out and was holding her hand and I had my answer. Hanna had loved them, begged for them, walked the streets of Pusan day and night trying to feed them, and she had taught them all they knew about Jesus. She had been the "cup of water" in Jesus' name to hundreds of these people.

Again my eye was drawn to that cross. It was no longer ugly or out of place. It had been transformed into something beautiful. "That old rugged cross so despised by the world, Has a wondrous attraction for me," and for thousands of others who know Jesus. Hanna Yang, like her sister Phoebe, was a "servant of the church" of our Lord.

The modern woman visiting the mission field will find a ministry. A distinct door of opportunity is open. There are business women's clubs, flower arrangement clubs, missionary societies, and many other organizations that would be pleased to hear her. She will bring a quality of warmth, a touch of the common things, and an abiding love that will set people at ease and make them more receptive to the gospel.

James Irwin, an astronaut who walked on the moon, and his wife came to Manila in November 1972. At a large banquet, Mr. Irwin showed a film of the moon trip, and then talked about his relationship to the Lord. It was a beautiful service. Finally, someone asked if we could hear from Mrs. Irwin. This gracious lady gave a testimony of praise. Then she talked about how God had blessed their home and their children. The crowd really seemed to respond to this. They were interested in the scientific moon exploration but they were not likely to go there. But the idea of God being in the home, of blessings and strength daily received, of little children and how she ministered to them, spoke to the needs of the people. Someone declared that Mr. Irwin challenged our minds; she spoke to our hearts.

One visiting lady, who was a seamstress, came and visited with the sewing shops. Another, interested in painting and art, had many opportunities to witness for Christ. Occupational kinship will break down barriers and melt cold hearts as we bear a witness to our fellow workers. That personal touch of wife to wife, mother to mother, and ironing board to ironing board, will speak a message understood most everywhere in the world.

The carpeted caverns of some hotel is no place to stay. The marketplace, the schools, shops, and homes need a witness. The modern Phoebes, "servants of the church," in the United States can extend that ministry to the uttermost part of the world.

Reflection # 12

Lieutenant Hiroo Onoda, a Japanese soldier, was sent to Lubang Island in the Philippines in 1944, as an expert in psychological warfare. He was told that the enemy would do all they could to deceive him and that he was not to be misled by propaganda.

Lieutenant Onoda spent the next thirty years on the island as a holdout. He refused to believe the war was over even when he heard the voice of his own father, taped and played from a heliocopter. He thought it was some type of psychological trick and refused to even acknowledge it. He declared: "My mission was uppermost on my mind. It was my support."

Finally, after a thirty-year cop-out, he was talked into surrendering by a Japanese reporter. He saw his first mirror in thirty years and jumped in amazement, not recognizing himself. He had lived among the islanders all this time but never really knew them. They are a warm, friendly people and a delight to know. To Onoda, they were always the enemy. He was sincere but sincerely deceived. I watched on Manila television as he laid his saber before President Ferdinand E. Marcos in a final act of capitulation. Inside I wept for a wasted life.

Is it not true that we can live among people for a week, or a month, or even a lifetime and never really know them? We can be deceived by the wrong information, or a closed mind. The love, joy, hopes, and despair of a nation never impressed the man. He knew much technical information about the island: its size, rainfall, tides, and defensible posi-

tions. But he knew nothing of that which mattered the most.

What a poor commentary on a servant of God when we can study a nation, serve among a people, know all the technical and sociological aspects and miss the most important thing. A nation's wealth is the people. Preconceived ideas, blind spots, and half-truths will lead us into a spiritual wilderness where we can wander forty years. Poor Onoda! The cup of love was all about him, but he never drank from it. When we love the people, the circumstances will be handled in the right manner.

12.
The Layman's Finest Ministry

The Florida layman worked as a postman. He saved his money and came to Korea to help in an evangelistic crusade. The language was new to him, but he spoke a language of love. He passed out tracts and spoke English to students and others who understood a little of his speech. He gave his testimony and preached with the aid of an interpreter. Several days after he left, I was talking with some of the local pastors and they mentioned him. They had really been impressed, not so much by his message, but by the other things he communicated. They were impressed by his willingness to work as a postman to earn money to come to Korea.

Once he had gone into a post office with the interpreter and shared his testimony with the whole staff. They loved it, and I do believe we got better mail service after that. His zeal to spread the Word and his enthusiasm impressed the men. Laymen had been touched because he "spoke to us." Several of the visiting pastors made a tremendous impact on the area, but the one they remembered the longest was the postman.

This nonprofessional approach is a great gift the layman adds to his ministry. He is a working man, taking his vacation time, using his own money, coming to share a witness with others. He preaches, gives his testimony, leads singing, and counsels with new converts. Often his speech is halting and he may not be a polished orator, but they listen. We feel much the same. It was an address by a laymen that touched so many of us at a recent Baptist convention. I think the finest testimony I ever heard was by a fisherman on the island of Cheju in Korea. He was poor, but this hardly distracted from his bearing. The Bible he carried was well-worn and he knew how to use it. The side frames of his glasses had worn away and he had looped string around his ears to hold them on. I remember that he spoke of being blessed by the Lord but I can't recall too much of his speech. However, he spoke to me through his sincerity, his position in life, and his concern for his church.

We are so prone to remember what a person is and his manner of speaking above that which is spoken. God uses the weak things of the world to confound the wise. It is when we realized our weakness that we lean heavily on God. All of us are at our best when we are ourselves. We are not trying to deceive, or impress, but earnestly trying to communicate God's love to these people. I heard a doctor make a very poor speech before the assembled staff and they loved him all the more. He didn't have to say much for he had been speaking to the people with his skillful hands, his loving concern for his patients, and by the late hours when they saw him in the hospital corridors. He had spoken loudest with his deeds.

The adaptability of the layman is a great witness. "What's a nice layman like you doing in a place like this" need not be asked of most laymen. They adapt to the circumstances and can make do with what is there. Complaining, great temper tantrums, and explosive expletives can injure a crusade quickly. Fortunately, there is little of this as the overseas guest quickly adapts and carries on an effective ministry.

The kindred occupation is another mark in the layman's favor. Postmen speak to postmen, auto mechanics speak a language understood to each other, and kindred professional men look forward to sharing ideas. It is communication that we seek and this is a big plus. Jim Irwin walked on the surface of the moon and testified that God was there. He spoke to us in Manila and said, "The same God who blessed me 240,000 miles away is with us tonight." A medical doctor accepted Christ that evening, declaring that "Any God who can span that space and still love me, then I want to know him." A high school band director had the time of his life visiting schools in the Philippines. Hundreds will stand to hear the testimonies of a touring basketball team. A homemaker telling about the difficulties of feeding her family and keeping it together will have an enraptured audience of mothers. This they understand and this message is one with which they can identify.

A great ministry of the visitor is encouragement. In the Bible, Barnabas was given a name that meant con-

solation or encouragement. Through the book of Acts
this wonderful man made a contribution that is still
remembered. He stood up for Paul in the Jerusalem
church and verified his testimony. In Antioch he was
overwhelmed with the work and set out to find Paul
to come and help with this ministry. Later, after Paul
rejected John Mark, Barnabas gave him a second
chance and history has vindicated the wisdom of that
move. Always hopeful, always encouraging others—
that was Barnabas.

Paul, in Romans 1:11–12 says, "For I long to see you,
that I may impart unto you some spiritual gift, to the
end ye may be established; That is, that I may be comforted together with you by the mutual faith both of
you and me." Note the words of encouragement in
this passage. He saw it as a two-way street; we give,
and we receive encouragement from the brethren. Do
we long to see them? Do we encourage them when
we do see them? Are we humble enough to receive
encouragement from them?

The layman's role of encouragement is most helpful
to the national and the mission work going on in his
country. He has enough problems without the layman
or missionary adding to the list. How delightful to be
encouraged! Maybe some good stiff questions would
help evaluate our ministry at this point.

1. Did I really listen to what he was trying to say?

2. Did he feel better for having been in my
presence?

3. Even though I didn't solve his problem did he
feel that at least I was concerned?

4. Did I reflect the spirit of Christ in my conversation in dealing with him?

5. Did he feel any less a man for having been with me? That is, did I respect him as an individual or was he just another brown-skinned, black-eyed fellow I had to deal with.

6. Did my manner of speaking and my attitude match up with my words?

All of these and a hundred more could be asked as we reflect on our dealings with people. Honesty is vital here. It's a shame to lead a person into believing we are going to write, or send him a gift, or perform a deed for him, when we know we aren't going to do it. It would be better to say, "No, I'm sorry, I can't do that," than to let him feel good for awhile and then be rudely disillusioned. We encourage others best by honesty and genuine concern.

The Report Back Home

Now the long trip is over. Jet lag makes you queasy for awhile but the world slowly falls back into its rightful place. You have your notes, slides, and souvenirs to share. The church family, your friends, and the pastor has shared in your trip, prayed for you while you were gone, and are eager to hear your report. Through the years the church has invested thousands of dollars in missions. They deserve a report. What will you say?

1. Tell it like it is. Let your slides be in color but your speech in black and white. There are many successes, but also failures; victories, but also defeats. The glamour and the idealism is there but also the muddy

roads, poverty pockets, and crowded ferryboats with smelly cargoes. Missionaries are not perfect, just trying to do the best they can. Nationals can be ornery, but some are still the salt of the earth.

2. Be factual. Out of every dollar the Foreign Mission Board receives, more than ninety cents reaches the field. Board personnel as well as the appointed missionaries are conscious of the sacrifice made as people have given the funds. Their desire is to see it used in this spirit with a deep sense of being a steward over the Lord's possessions. The Southern Baptist Annual (your pastor has a copy) will give you the information on any of the eighty-three countries where we have work. The number of missionaries, the amount spent there, the number of churches and membership will be listed.

3. If slides are presented, don't try to use more than thirty or forty. You can't show them all and it will take forty minutes to show thirty slides and give a brief explanation. Congregations will grow weary if you make it a travelogue.

4. Be optimistic. If this proves difficult, in light of what you have seen and heard, then please discuss the negatives with the missionaries or with Foreign Mission Board personnel. If you are still persuaded that the negative view is to be presented, then at least you can also present the position of the Foreign Mission Board along with it.

Often, sharp questions will center around the use of finances. The Cooperative Program is not perfect, but it is still one of the better plans of any denomination for being a channel through which flows the gifts of

35,000 churches to our missionary enterprises. The Lottie Moon offering may not appeal to some people, but it touches the hearts of more Baptists and the response is greater than any similar offering in the world today.

There is much to be optimistic about. We have a God who is able, a commission to spread the Word through out the world, and dedicated people willing to give and go. There is so much for which we can praise our Lord. Melinda Rankin, first Protestant missionary to Mexico said, "The word discouragement is not in the dictionary of the kingdom of heaven." Melville's classic line, "a damp, drizzly November in my soul" may have expressed his feelings, but it is a warm spring day in the mission world. "The sunlight is glancing, O'er armies advancing" is the scene for dedicated Christians determined to obey the Lord.

I keenly feel that this is an area where the layman can make a real impact for Christ. People have heard it from visiting missionaries or the pastor, but now, one of their own laymen tells of the victories being won. His attitude will be reflected in the future mission activities of his church. What a glorious privilege and such a vast responsibility now in your hands.

5. Make it plain to the people that they are having part in a ministry that is worldwide. Connect the week by week giving of the church with the Cooperative Program and the varied ministries that you have seen. It will be a great temptation to say, "I've been there and I've seen the great need of the hospital, or the school, or the chapel, and I want our church to do something special for those missionaries out there."

Your spirit is commendable and most appreciated, however, it is the week by week giving to all our mission program that will help those missionaries "out there." Their greatest need is not specially designated gifts, but the prayer support of your congregation plus a constant stream of giving. Every time you give to your church budget you are helping the nationals and the missionaries. This kind of help is more meaningful and lasting than the "spur of the moment" special offerings.

Think of what it would mean if our congregations were trained to see the offering as a time of worship in which they were teaching, healing, and ministering to needs around the globe. This could revolutionize the Sunday offering.

6. As you encouraged the workers on the field, so encourage those in your home church. They need it too. They haven't been in a 747 over the Pacific. They have been behind a counter in a hardware store, or driving a truck across the interstate. They don't need to be "brow-beaten" because some Baptists give so little or do so little. This will hardly encourage them to do more. Bewildering statistics on population growth, the decline of church life in some areas, or the growth of Islam in another, is not likely to "speed them on their way." Did you ever hear a person speak, and when he finished you felt like you had the best icebox on the market, but everyone wanted a refrigerator? Our people are doing a lot of mission work in spite of adversities and inflation. While it may not be as much as we could do, it is more than we have ever done

before. We are growing, our work is advancing, and our people need to be encouraged in this. The layman's finest ministry may be in *encouraging his people* as he returns to report.

The layman is also in position to keep in touch with the missionaries and nationals on the fields where he has visited. The old "pen pal" idea has been revived, and it is nice to hear from some person who lives ten thousand miles away. You can share experiences together, invite the missionary to your home while he is on furlough, and, in general, keep a fresh report before your church. This has been most meaningful in ham radio operators who were in touch with Guatemala, Mexico, and Ecuador in some of the recent disasters. They were able to share firsthand reports with the various mission boards, denominational papers, and their home church. It doesn't cost much to mail a letter, it doesn't take a lot of time to write it, but the blessings it can bring are tremendous.

Frequently an enlarged ministry comes to the pastor or lay worker who has visited mission fields. He is invited to associational meetings, conventions, and retreats. His optimistic, encouraging report will give a vital push to our total mission endeavor. The willingness to go, to share, is incumbent upon those who can challenge people in the cause of Christ. The active participation of laymen in the church today is one of the most thrilling things on the mission horizon. In the field of witnessing, sharing, and faithful service, the layman is claiming his place, and for this we give thanks.

Appendix A
A New Look at Some Old Fallacies

1. All missionaries are perfect saints. This is usually debunked at the airport or in the first traffic jam. Most of them are fine Christians, but they are not too fond of being placed on a pedestal with the golden halo.

2. Missionaries are bound to be doing a good work because they are on the mission field. American businessmen, embassy personnel, and often a large number of military personnel are on the mission field too. Distance from the homeland adds very little to a person's dedication to Christ. Crossing the ocean never made a man more of a missionary. Those who are zealous and enthusiastic workers in the United States of America will be that way on the field. A miserable, frustrated missionary can do more harm than good. It's the quiet, but determined, conviction that this is where God wants him that will keep a missionary laboring effectively.

3. That a lot of activity means a lot of work is being done. He was up by 5:30 A.M. trying to get a kerosene stove going. There was barely time for breakfast, as he had to drive the children across town for school. The plumbers were coming to work on the pump and

he needed to be there. On the way back he dashed into a tailor shop where they were making a suit for him.

Harassing the plumbers took the rest of the morning, and the early part of the afternoon was used in a committee meeting to decide orientation policies for visitors coming to the field. He had to rush out early for it was his week to drive the school kids. One tire was flat on the vehicle.

His wife met him at the gate to say the maid had plugged the 115 volt freezer into a 220 volt socket and the house was filled with smoke. Five minutes later, he had to rush the gardener to the hospital to have his foot sewn up; he had cut it with the hoe. Many times he had complained about long handled American hoes. The correct type had a two foot handle. It was dark when he came back. His seventh grader had to have two pieces of poster paper for school the next day. He took off, spinning gravel upon the garage wall, fussed at the old gateman for being so slow in getting the gate opened, and lectured the clerk on how to wrap poster paper.

At 8:00 o'clock that night, two missionaries came over to discuss plans for the new Baptist building. They left at 10:30. By 11:00 o'clock he tumbled into bed saying, "Thank you, Lord, for a great day of missionary service."

Not all days are that way, but few missionaries escape having some like that. Add a Bible class or two, a trip to visit a church, or a pastor's conference and the picture could be duplicated in many fields. Suffice it to note that activity is not synonymous with mission work.

4. That missionaries are satisfied with the bare minimum of worldly goods. A few are, but most of them are just like Christian workers in the rest of the world.

5. That missionaries can get by on practically nothing; they really live by faith. Only partially true. They still have to pay for food when guests come in and maybe stay a week. Unless they are on "mission business" it will have to come from the missionary's pocket. They do live by faith. Faith in God, and faith that their fellow workers will pay their share.

6. That the missionary gets a paid vacation one year out of every five. True, he gets a furlough, but it could hardly qualify as a vacation. Some have to return to the field to get some rest. They are paid full salary while on furlough. However, the expenses of closing down one home, opening another, and then reversing the procedure a year later is quite expensive.

Appendix B
Timely Tips for World Travelers

1. Be communicative. If you are going for a conference, or revival crusade, write the Foreign Mission Board and inform them of plans and procedures. They have much valuable information that will assist you in various overseas trips. The mission will have to coordinate crusades with national conventions and church leaders. It will take time and effort, but will pay great dividends. Send copies of all letters to the people involved and keep a copy for your files.

2. Make sure the missionaries know when you are coming. They need to know the date, airline and flight number, and how many are coming with you. International airports are usually crowded but they can be lonely places if no one is there to meet you.

3. Make your talents known. Singing, guitar, or other musical ability, doing magic tricks, basketball star, or whatever, it can help draw people who would not come otherwise. It is good to let the missionary know what you can do, and know what he expects of you.

4. Travel light when possible. You are not likely to need your entire wardrobe. Light wash and wear

for the tropics. If in doubt, write the mission chairman, or check with a furloughing missionary from that field.

5. Record your trip. Camera, tape recorder, and a journal all can be used to good advantage. Write down your impressions, the list of people you meet, and interesting things that happen. The dullest pencil is usually more accurate than the sharpest mind.

6. Some pastors and laymen have found it helpful to call their home church during a worship service. By using an amplified telephone he can communicate a personal message from the mission field that will be meaningful without costing a great deal. Emphasis could be placed on the need of mission volunteers and giving to your mission program through the local church budget.

7. Discriminate reading will enhance your value to the mission field, and be a personal experience that you will enjoy. History, travel adventures, biographies of great personalities, even fiction will help you to understand the people and the country. The Foreign Mission Board has some excellent pamphlets entitled, *Southern Baptist Laymen on Assignment Abroad, A Dedication Service for Laymen Going Abroad,* and *Unofficial Missionaries.* Your church library or nearest bookstore will have books on missionaries, mission trends, and all the more recent changes in mission work.

8. Get a list of the missionaries working in the country where you are going and begin to pray for them by name and for the ministry there. The Mission Board can give you a list or it can be obtained from the mission

chairman. This will enable you to begin your ministry long before reaching the field and to continue it after leaving.

9. Deal frankly with your host. If in doubt, inquire about paying for food or lodging wherever you are. The orientation will usually cover this, but should you fail to understand, then ask someone. A small hotel bill may be equal to a month's budget of the church where you will be preaching, and it would greatly strain the church or the missionary to pay for it. Most of this is spelled out in the crusade planning, but often there are some embarrassing situations when the guest visitors do not know what is the best procedure.

10. Take advantage of your "foreignness" and use it creatively. Much of the world is hungry for the English language, and students may approach you on the street. You will quickly be invited or admitted to places where the local pastor has never been. Colleges, radio and television stations, various interviews, and civic clubs will be happy to hold out the welcome mat. If you are in a crusade make sure your host pastor is also invited, for he can continue the ministry after you are gone.

Your differences in color, height, size, and even education can be used as bridges that will create a warm atmosphere for sharing your message. The people will enjoy laughing with you.

11. Try not to reveal your shock, dismay, or disgust at some of their habits and ways that are so different. They would probably feel that way about some of your habits. I recall, attending my first WMU Convention

in Korea, they announced a "fan dance." Total shock was registered on my face until about twelve elderly ladies, dressed in colorful costumes, came out and did a beautiful Korean folk dance.

12. Keep your purpose in mind. As a witness for our Lord, you would want to do nothing that would lessen the effect of your ministry. Our purpose is sharing the lovely story of Jesus Christ, the eternal message of the Son of God, which will bring great joy and peace into the troubled lives of the world today. Vast are the responsibilities, and great is the reward for those who are faithful in this task.